How-To

MARIJUANA

HOW-TO

MARIJUANA

A Step-by-Step Guide
to Medical Marijuana

CAROL S. BOTT, RN
Chemical Dependency Nurse

iUniverse, Inc.
New York Lincoln Shanghai

How-To Marijuana
A Step-by-Step Guide to Medical Marijuana

Copyright © 2007 by Carol S. Bott, RN

iUniverse books may be ordered through booksellers or by contacting:

iUniverse
2021 Pine Lake Road, Suite 100
Lincoln, NE 68512
www.iuniverse.com
1-800-Authors (1-800-288-4677)

Because of the dynamic nature of the Internet, any Web addresses or links contained in this book may have changed since publication and may no longer be valid.

The information, ideas, and suggestions in this book are not intended as a substitute for professional medical advice. Before following any suggestions contained in this book, you should consult your personal physician. Neither the author nor the publisher shall be liable or responsible for any loss or damage allegedly arising as a consequence of your use or application of any information or suggestions in this book.

ISBN: 978-0-595-45086-2 (pbk)
ISBN: 978-0-595-69191-3 (cloth)
ISBN: 978-0-595-89397-3 (ebk)

Printed in the United States of America

To the sheriff and the district attorney of El Dorado County, California, as well as to their staff and officers, and to the El Dorado County American Alliance for Medical Cannabis, for working with instead of against each other, and for striving to put compassion and the people and laws of the state of California first, not last. You all make me very proud to live in El Dorado County.

Contents

Acknowledgments

I wish to thank Jon Moore for beautiful photography, freely given; Jon's friendship is a fascinating adventure. I also wish to thank my friend, Dave Bishop, for sharing his ideas and concepts and allowing me to incorporate them in my book. He has been a tremendous help and support. My friend, Bob, came up with a wonderful title for the book and receives my profound gratitude. Thanks are also due to Judy Ryland, a dear friend who taught me topical preparations and generously shared hard-earned wisdom. Thanks to N for her recipes; her oatmeal cookies are *delicious*. Thank you to all the patients and their families who have worked with me and taught me. Heartfelt thanks to Philip Denney, MD, for inspiring me to write this book in the first place, and for helping me clarify patients' issues. Last, but definitely not least, fervent gratitude to my husband, Terry, for patiently assisting his computer-illiterate wife with this book. Knowing each and every one of you, plus all the others that there is not enough room to mention, is a joy, a pleasure, and an honor. This book would not exist without you. Thank you!

The reference sources I used must also be mentioned. If the authors of those books and articles had not already done their work, I couldn't have done mine. I owe them all a debt of gratitude. I feel that special mention is due to Fred Gardner. He not only took time from his busy life to offer support and check references: he also produced *O'Shaughnessy's*. If Fred had not put years of effort into this excellent and professional publication, and if he and the physicians who work with him had not documented the results of their work with medical cannabis patients over the past ten years, there would have been much less medical information for me to compile. We are all the richer for their efforts.

Preface

Part one contains a compilation of recent and historical medical research and anecdotal evidence, arranged in a question-and-answer format. The questions are those that in my experience are frequently being asked by medical cannabis patients and their families. The table of contents at the front of the book lists each question. I have included a bibliography of my reference sources at the end of the first part. I strongly recommend it as a continued reading list for those who are interested in greater detail or who want to learn more.

Examples of situations in which medical cannabis was beneficial follow some of the questions. These stories and the characters within them are entirely fictional. They were created by compiling patients' reports and case histories, including my own.

Once I began working within the medical cannabis community, I discovered that many patients don't really know how to prepare or grow cannabis to obtain the best quality of plant and therapeutic effect. Therefore, parts two and three contain directions for growing cannabis outdoors, including how to start your own seedlings or clones, how to make your own compost, how to determine gender, and how to harvest, cure, and dry the cannabis herb. I also teach you how to make edible and topical preparations. I've provided step-by-step, detailed instructions, and have collected recipes from the best cooks and natural healers I know, along with documenting my own recipes and preparations. I've kept the instructions simple because you really can do this simply. You do not have to hold a PhD to prepare and grow excellent-quality medical cannabis.

Chapter eight concludes this book with a discussion of the legal issues to be considered prior to making any personal decisions about the use of medical cannabis.

Introduction

Marijuana, hemp, Mary Jane, reefer, pot, weed, ganja: all of these and many more are colloquial names for *Cannabis sativa*. Cannabis is an annual herb that has been used throughout human history as sacrament, and for medicine, oil, food, and fiber. In fact, the term *sativa* means cultivated or useful, as opposed to wild. The oldest confirmed use of cannabis was in China in 3750 BC (Conrad 1997, 14). The cannabis plant, like the apple, potato, and rose, has evolved alongside the human race, reflecting our desires and needs. We have both affected and been affected by it.

Over time, many different strains of cannabis have been developed to meet its wide variety of uses. Medicinal or therapeutic applications are multiple, and include asthma, glaucoma, Crohn's disease, tumors, cancer chemotherapy, migraines, chronic pain, epilepsy, arthritis, insomnia, depression, posttraumatic stress disorder (PTSD), multiple sclerosis, AIDS, and Alzheimer's disease. Recently, research has focused on the newly discovered endocannabinoid system, which includes cannabinoid receptor sites within our bodies and brains. These sites are tailored to receive cannabinoids manufactured by our own bodies and appear to be deeply involved with regulating the overall balance, or homeostasis, of all of our systems.

Unfortunately, in our modern era, we've lost much that we once knew. This is especially true in the various areas of natural medicines and treatment approaches, and nowhere more so than with cannabis. Although virtually all anecdotal and research evidence indicates nothing but benefit from *Cannabis sativa*, this healing herb has been the victim of a great deal of misinformation and misunderstanding.

As a registered nurse who worked in the field of chemical dependency, I personally observed the harm done not just by recreational street drugs such as heroin, crank, and cocaine, but also by alcohol, tobacco, and prescription medications. Cannabis not only does no harm, it is one of the most beneficial, healing, and balancing herbs I've ever encountered. I feel it is vital that misinformation be addressed, the truth be told, and innocent, suffering, and dying people no longer be denied the relief and help cannabis can give them when used appropriately. So, I wrote this book.

Marijuana: medicine or menace? Let's investigate the history and evidence and set the record straight!

PART I

Marijuana: Medicine or Menace?

Chapter One

Questions and Answers

Q: Why is cannabis illegal?

Before I even start to answer this question, any discussion of the political history of cannabis must mention the book, *The Emperor Wears No Clothes*, by Jack Herer (refer to the list of references). Much of my answer was compiled from that book, which is an extensive and exhaustive review of the history of cannabis medicine and industrial hemp. Please note that whole books have been written in answer to this query. I enthusiastically and wholeheartedly refer you to those books and other sources in my references if you desire more detailed information.

Cannabis has been illegal in this country since December 1937. Prior to this, it was one of the primary medicines in the American pharmacopoeia, and was widely prescribed to all ages for a variety of medical conditions. It was also offered in candy and was available in hashish smoking parlors, open in every major American city by 1883.

Cannabis hemp was heavily cultivated by American farmers for fiber, food, and oil, as is still being done in other countries today. It was a major base upon which American industry rested. Unfortunately, cannabis was so versatile and valuable that it threatened to reduce the profits of large timber companies, such as Hearst Paper Manufacturing Division, part of Randolph Hearst's holdings, as well as the newly developing, petroleum-based industries dominated by DuPont. In the mid-1930s, at the same time as modern equipment was appearing to deal with harvesting and processing industrial hemp, DuPont patented processes to manufacture plastics from oil and coal and paper from wood pulp. Mr. Hearst, DuPont, and such allies as Andrew Mellon of the Mellon Bank of Pittsburgh, stood to lose a lot of money if cannabis continued to be grown and used instead of the products they were selling.

Subsequently, Andrew Mellon, acting as President Hoover's secretary of the treasury, appointed Harry J. Anslinger (his future nephew-in-law) head of the newly created Federal Bureau of Narcotics, now the Drug Enforcement Administration (DEA). A pogrom of lies using the term *marijuana*, Mexican slang for cannabis, appealed to racism and fear and succeeded in outlawing cannabis, partly because those who would have protested did not realize that the "dreaded killer drug marijuana" was actually just *Cannabis sativa*.

Despite horrified and impassioned last-minute protests by the American Medical Association and the National Oil Seed Institute, among others, cannabis became illegal in the United States of America in 1937. Since its prohibition, the cotton, alcohol, tobacco, pharmaceutical, and law enforcement industries have joined older anti-cannabis factions and the federal government to promote the continued prohibition and suppression of cannabis information and research.

"In America our history gets taken away from us and we don't even know it. We're taught that systematic falsifications only happen in other countries, where individual rights are not respected and the masses are impotent and cynical. Well, it happens here, too" (*O'Shaughnessy's,* Spring 2006, 39).

Q: What conditions does cannabis treat?

Under California law, per Proposition 215, a person may use medical cannabis, with a physician's recommendation, for "the treatment of cancer, anorexia, AIDS, chronic pain, spasticity, glaucoma, arthritis, migraine, or any other illness for which marijuana provides relief." Other states that have legalized cannabis for medical use have instituted different parameters. For information on medical cannabis laws in other states, go to NORML's Web site: http://www.norml.org/; or,

go to the Web site of Americans for Safe Access (ASA): http://
www.safeaccessnow.org/.

In reality, cannabis helps a multitude of conditions and com-
plaints. Because of the way the California law reads, physicians in the
state have had a unique opportunity to participate in what has been
termed "a vast public health experiment." The Winter/Spring 2007
issue of *O'Shaughnessy's* contains a survey of eighteen California physicians who practice cannabis medicine. The doctors reported treat-
ing many conditions successfully with cannabis. These included
cancer and related symptoms, anorexia, AIDS, chronic pain of all
kinds, spasticity, arthritis, migraines, emotional and mental disorders, intestinal disorders, chemical dependency, diabetes symptoms,
kidney problems, liver failure, adrenal diseases, airway diseases, obe-
sity, epilepsy, multiple sclerosis, and skin disorders, among many
others. Conditions physicians felt were unusual included Gulf War
syndrome, skin reactions from Agent Orange, esophageal achalasia,
Marfan's syndrome, and violent autism. (Cannabis is looking
extremely promising as a treatment for autism and attention deficit
disorders.)

For more detailed information, I recommend *O'Shaughnessy's*
Winter/Spring 2007 issue. The newspaper can be contacted by
phone at 415-305-4758 or by e-mail at journal@ccrmg. Their mail-
ing address is Post Office Box 490, Alameda, California, 94501.

Q: What conditions will allow me to qualify for a medical cannabis recommendation?

A recommendation for medical cannabis in California is provided by
a physician or osteopath and is good for one year at a time. For information on medical cannabis rules in other states, go to http://
www.norml.org/or to http://www.safeaccessnow.org/. Hopefully,
you won't develop a disease or condition that will require medical

intervention, but if you do, there is no specific diagnosis or title that will guarantee a recommendation for the use of medical cannabis. Normally, during your consultation with a cannabis medicine specialist in California, the physician reviews your medical records, including what other therapies you've already tried, conducts his or her own physical and/or psychiatric examination, then issues a recommendation for the use of medical cannabis if he or she agrees that this is an appropriate therapy in your case. At that time, the doctor can also help you determine the dose you need and can advise on other delivery methods, such as using a vaporizer, ingesting cannabis, or applying it topically. Some medical cannabis patients possess recommendations from their own personal physician and a cannabis specialist.

Q: What are Proposition 215 and SB 420?

In 1996, voters in California passed Proposition 215, dubbed the Compassionate Use Act of 1996. This initiative allows patients with a physician's recommendation to legally use medical cannabis in the state of California, although this use remains a federal offense and cannot pass state lines. Proposition 215 also allows for cultivation and caregiver functions. California Senate Bill 420 (SB 420/HS 11362.7) was passed in 2003 by the California legislature in an attempt to facilitate and clarify implementation of Proposition 215. SB 420 makes provisions for a voluntary ID card program, establishes threshold limits on allowable quantities of live cannabis plants and processed cannabis, provides for the possibility of collective and cooperative grows, and extends the power of cannabis recommendations to California osteopaths. Other states that have legalized cannabis for medical use have established their own guidelines. For information on medical cannabis rules in other states: http://www.safeaccessnow.org/or http://www.norml.org/.

Q: Will legalization encourage teenage use?

The simple answer to this is no. An article in the Autumn 2005 *O'Shaughnessy's*, page eight, quotes Katherine O'Keefe and Mitch Earleywine: "Nine years after the passage of the nation's first state medical marijuana law … a considerable body of data shows that no state with a medical marijuana law has experienced an increase in youth marijuana use since their law's enactment. All have reported overall decreases of more than the national average decrease—exceeding 50 percent in some age groups—strongly suggesting that enactment of state medical marijuana laws does not increase teen marijuana use." And, remember, it has been commonly established that Holland has experienced considerably reduced cannabis usage among adolescents since decriminalization, which I assume removed the attraction of engaging in a proscribed activity.

Q: Is cannabis a gateway drug?

Tom O'Connell, MD, reported on an ongoing study he has been conducting in California, using applicants who have applied for medical cannabis recommendations under Proposition 215. Dr. O'Connell concluded that results of his study so far cast "great doubt on the validity of any 'gateway' role for cannabis. It supports the opposite interpretation" (*O'Shaughnessy's*, Autumn 2005, 8).

In their report of March 1999, the Institute of Medicine (IOM) found no evidence that cannabis use was a risk factor for progression to use of other substances. They stated, "The gateway theory is a social theory." They felt that the legal status of cannabis was the cause of any problems, not the pharmacological qualities of the herb, itself. They concluded, "In other words, the real 'gateway' to hard drugs is marijuana prohibition, not marijuana!" (Herer 2000, 132). And don't forget: prior to prohibition in 1937, cannabis was widely prescribed by American physicians to all ages without any reported harm.

Not only is there no valid evidence that cannabis is a gateway drug, all indications are that it can actually function as a harm reduction substitute for many individuals. This means that they use cannabis instead of alcohol or whatever other drugs they are addicted to. Jeffrey Hergenrather, MD, stated, "People who were formerly dependent on alcohol, opiates, amphetamines, and other addictive drugs have had their lives changed when substituting with cannabis" (*O'Shaughnessy's*, Winter/Spring 2007, 1).

Michael's Story

Michael swallowed the last dregs of his cooling coffee, watching from his back porch as the stormy day faded into evening. Suddenly, the sky cleared to tatters and puffs of clouds, revealing glimpses of bright azure pierced with the day's final, golden shafts.

"That sky's a reminder that the light is always there, no matter how overwhelming things seem—just like my life over the past few years," Michael mused to himself. "Five years ago, I sure wasn't watching the sun go down from my own porch. I'd been fired for being drunk on the job and was really busy drinking my life away. I was in the process of losing everything—thank God for recovery!"

Michael recalled that during his downward spiral into severe alcoholism, he had mostly just stayed drunk. One afternoon, he awakened, hung over and stinking once more, on his friend Jonathan's couch. He was already feeling shaky and needed a drink. But, to Michael's horror, instead of handing him a beer as he usually did, Jonathan passed him a cannabis cigarette. "I don't keep beer or anything here anymore, dude," he said. "I quit drinking 'cause it was messing me up so bad. My old lady wasn't gonna let me see the kids anymore. I found out that if I just smoked a little pot, I could stay away from the drink."

Michael remembered cursing foully, but he smoked the joint in desperation, hoping it would steady him until he could get some booze. To his complete shock, after he used the cannabis, he had noticed that he felt steadier and didn't want a drink quite as badly (though that certainly didn't stop him from drinking anyway).

Although cannabis was not a panacea, and Michael did not stop drinking immediately, he gradually found himself substituting cannabis for alcohol more and more often. He was functioning and feeling better; alcohol cravings were reduced. He was regaining lost weight, and his health was improving. Michael was able to think clearly again and sought help from a local twelve-step program. After about a year, he stopped drinking completely, and he never looked back. Cannabis, sobriety skills, and consistent participation in a twelve-step group allowed Michael to regain his livelihood, his home, his health, and his self-respect.

Q: Is cannabis addictive?

According to *Dorland's Illustrated Medical Dictionary, Twenty-sixth Edition*, 1985, page twenty-nine, for a substance to be considered addictive, it must: create an overwhelming compulsion to continue using it and do anything necessary to obtain it; create a tendency to increase the dose; create psychological and usually physical dependence; and have a detrimental effect on the individual user and society. Cannabis does not fit this profile, although many pharmaceutical medications do, as do alcohol, tobacco, and recreational street drugs.

Cannabis has been used by the human race as sacrament, medicine, food, and fiber without harm throughout the ages. There has been no recorded death from cannabis overdose or toxicity. The

IOM report (March 1999) found no significant addictive potential for cannabis (Herer 2000, 132). Fred Gardner, in his report on a meeting of the International Cannabinoid Research Society (ICRS), stated, "Ethan Russo of GW Pharmaceuticals showed that abrupt cessation of a medicinal cannabis extract was not associated with a withdrawal syndrome" (*O'Shaughnessy's,* Autumn 2005, 10).

Our own bodies contain an endocannabinoid system, with receptors tailored for specific cannabinoid molecules: this is the reason cannabis works. The development of tolerance and subsequent dosage increases does not occur with cannabis, as it does with prescription opiates, narcotics, and major tranquilizers, as well as with alcohol, tobacco, and street drugs such as heroin, cocaine, and methamphetamine (crank). There are no physical withdrawal symptoms; neither are there withdrawal-induced psychoses.

William Eidlman, MD, and R. Lee Hamilton, EDD, PhD, UCLA researchers, stated, "What the world needs now is intelligent legalization of cannabis hemp, especially for medical intervention" (Herer 2000, 249).

Q: Is cannabis stronger and therefore more dangerous today?

Potency is primarily a factor of heredity. Cannabis has not suddenly grown inherently stronger, but growers are becoming increasingly skilled at maximizing its genetic potential. Cannabis contains over sixty active compounds. Delta-9-tetrahydrocannabinol (THC) is the primary psychoactive ingredient in cannabis. The percentage of THC determines cannabis' potency and can vary from as low as 0.001 percent in cannabis hemp plants bred for fiber (Conrad 1997, 51) to over 10 percent in extremely potent, high-quality medicinal cannabis (http://www.medicalcannabis.com/, *Marijuana Myths: Ten Most Common Concerns About Cannabis*). THC content also varies by the part of the plant used and by each individual plant. Unseeded, mature female buds are the most medicinal. The psychotropic and medicinal effects of THC are moderated by the other cannabinoids present, as well as by other components, such as terpenes. Study of this synergistic interaction is in its infancy.

Finally, remember that cannabis has a very wide safety margin. There is no record of serious cannabis overdose. In fact, an article on the Patients Out of Time Web site (http://www.medical cannabis.com/) states that one would have to smoke fifteen hundred pounds of cannabis in fifteen minutes to cause a lethal overdose—a physically impossible feat (*Marijuana Myths: Ten Most Common Concerns About Cannabis*).

Holly's Story

Holly wiped the sweat from her forehead with the back of her gloved hand, spreading mud down to her nose, and contemplated the row of roses she'd just pruned. It was certainly easier to garden, hike, and do all the other things she loved when she didn't weigh one hundred and ninety pounds! The fifty-pound weight gain caused by the anti-depressant medication her doctor had prescribed had definitely *not* relieved her depression. When Holly finally figured out that it was the medication causing the uncontrolled increase in her normal weight, she stopped taking it. She remembered thinking, "Now, I'm depressed *and* obese! Not much of a help." (*Warning:* some antidepressant medications must not be abruptly terminated. Consult your physician if you want to stop taking one.)

Despite years of counseling and recovery work, Holly's childhood had left scars. She suffered from PTSD, regularly experiencing the depression, anxiety, insomnia, and nightmares that usually accompany this disorder. No amount of counseling or personal work could completely eliminate these challenges.

Holly did what she could. Now that she was off the medication, she could lose weight. She resumed hiking, which helped the pounds come off. She worked in her gardens and appreciated the beauty surrounding her mountain home. She came out of seclusion and reconnected with friends, resuming a social life.

But Holly did not sleep well; neither did she experience any real relief from anxiety or nightmares. At least, she didn't until a friend who was active in the local medical cannabis community gave her some cookies baked with cannabis butter and suggested she eat some before bed, cautioning her to start with about a quarter of a cookie. Her friend explained that she could adjust upward or downward over a period of time, until she determined her dose.

Holly tried it, gradually settling on two cookies at bedtime. She found that she could sleep through the night most nights, and she did not remember her dreams. She awoke clear-headed and felt better than she had in a long time. And she was able to continue to lose the excess weight!

After joining the medical cannabis group in her community, Holly proceeded, with great enthusiasm, to learn all she could about the herb. She learned how to grow it, cook with it, and make topical preparations. She learned to use a vaporizer instead of smoking. She discovered that a couple of puffs of cannabis vapor could head off an incipient anxiety attack and help her stay balanced. Holly still needed and regularly utilized her recovery and coping skills; cannabis did not solve all her life's problems. Cannabis did, however, improve the overall quality of her life. It allowed her to sleep at night and enjoy herself while awake, without the serious, harmful side effects that accompanied the use of pharmaceutical medications.

Q: Is cannabis dangerous because it stays in your system for thirty days?

This concept misrepresents the actual facts. According to Thomas Ungerbieder, MD, Donald Tashkin, MD, and Tod Mikuriya, MD, the active ingredients in cannabis are used up in a few hours, after the first or second pass through the liver (Herer 2000, 111). The inert metabolites that are left then attach themselves to fatty deposits for elimination over a period of time. This is a perfectly normal and natural process. It is these harmless and inert metabolites that urine drug testing is detecting.

Q: How can dosage be controlled when using the natural cannabis plant?

Remember: cannabis is nontoxic, with no record of death by overdose. Dosage varies by the individual, the condition being treated, and by the strain and quality of the medicine itself, as well as by the route of administration.

When medicating by smoking or vaporizing, the effect manifests within minutes and lasts for two to four hours. It is extremely easy and simple to inhale only enough to achieve the desired relief or therapeutic effect.

Ingesting cannabis causes the compounds to be released more slowly as they are digested. This effect can take up to two hours to onset and can last four to eight hours or longer. It's better to begin by consuming a small amount, gradually increasing the dosage over time until the desired therapeutic effect is obtained.

Topical applications are useful in reducing pain, inflammation, and some skin conditions. The cannabis root, which contains absolutely no THC and is not psychoactive, is full of anti-inflammatory compounds. It can be used to prepare liniments and topical oils that help reduce muscle and joint pain. The rest of the plant also has anti-inflammatory and antimicrobial properties (*O'Shaughnessy's,* Winter/Spring 2007, 9, 11–15).

According to Chris Conrad, one would have to consume a minimum of one to two pounds of top-quality cannabis in about two hours to even possibly be in any danger. He stated, "In short, a potentially lethal dose of THC is several thousand times more than its effective medical dose" (Conrad 1997, 191).

That's much safer than many common pharmaceutical medications and definitely safer than alcohol and tobacco!

Q: Why use cannabis instead of Marinol?

Marinol (dronabinol is the generic form) is synthetic THC. It is available by prescription and can be obtained from a pharmacy.

A large part of cannabis' medicinal value derives from the synergistic interactions of all of its active components (in other words, from the whole herb). Treatment with Marinol has had very mixed results. Many patients are unable to tolerate Marinol or to establish a consistently therapeutic dose. Without the mitigating and balancing effects of such compounds as cannabidiol (CBD), which has multiple medical uses of its own, THC (not to mention *synthetic* THC) tends to cause increased problems and side effects, such as dysphoria (mood disturbance) and tachycardia (rapid heart beat).

In his report on the International Cannabinoid Research Society conference, Mr. Gardner, who edits *O'Shaughnessy's,* stated, "Several studies supported the notion that cannabis is more than simply THC. This should be no surprise, given the number of people who consume medical cannabis yet cannot tolerate Marinol" (*O'Shaughnessy's,* Autumn 2005, 10). The simple fact is that a synthetically-produced single compound is unlikely to be as efficacious as the whole, natural plant. We are not yet wiser than Mother Nature.

Q: Doesn't cannabis contain hundreds of compounds?

While it is true that the cannabis plant contains about four hundred compounds, many of these same compounds are also found in other herbs and vegetables, such as tomatoes. And don't forget that tobacco cigarettes contain over seven hundred chemicals, of which almost all are nonbeneficial (Conrad 1997, 146). Approximately sixty unique compounds called cannabinoids are primarily responsible for the medicinal qualities of cannabis. Cannabinoids and our body's endocannabinoid system, with its receptor sites for cannabinoid molecules, are still under study, but antimicrobial and anti-inflammatory properties, among many others, have already been demonstrated (*O'Shaughnessy's,* Winter/Spring 2007, 9, 11–15). It is cannabis' inherent complexity that has made it so useful and valuable throughout the history of the human race.

Daniel's Story

Daniel realized that he was too busy vomiting to pay much attention to the back pain he had been attempting to relieve by taking the pain medication that was now nauseating him. This situation had become all too familiar to him since he had injured his lower back two years before. "Somehow," he thought to himself wryly, "I don't think this is quite what I had in mind by pain relief." As the spasms eased, he collapsed back onto his heels. Unfortunately, he had obviously found yet another pain medication that he could no longer tolerate. Daniel wiped the cold sweat off his face with a shaky hand. The prescription drugs were all so hard on him that he couldn't take any of them for very long. And he was so tired of being unproductive, not to mention struggling to pay for all that stuff his doctor kept prescribing. His wife and kids were trying, but this was not how any of them had envisioned their lives. "I'd rather not live at all than keep living this way," he thought despairingly.

He wasn't actually suicidal yet, but Daniel was depressed and discouraged; his self-esteem was nonexistent. "This isn't working. I've got to do something different. The back pain isn't going away—I've *got* to find another way to deal with this!" Daniel climbed painfully to his feet to clean out his mouth and discovered, shoved in the drawer where he kept his toothpaste, the cannabis cigarette that his friend, Barb, had left with him the other day.

"Those narcotics and stuff you're taking are just making everything worse!" she'd declared. "*Please* try cannabis. I'm going to leave you this joint. You smoke it next time the pills don't help, and you see what happens!"

Daniel had heard it all from Barb before, and he didn't want to argue. "My back may hurt, but I take medicine, not drugs," he had muttered defiantly. He had shoved the joint in the bathroom drawer and forgotten about it—until now. Now, the medicine was *not* working, and he was desperate.

Daniel smoked the joint. As he smoked, he realized his muscles were relaxing; he was feeling a little happier and less nauseated. The pain wasn't gone, but it was reduced, and it didn't seem as important; he felt distanced from it. Maybe pot *was* medicine!

Daniel finished that joint. Then he called Barb to tell her just how right she'd been. He continued to use cannabis medically and was able to gradually reduce his need for many other medications; he completely cut out some. He was no longer dependent on narcotics. His digestive system functioned again, he was able to sleep, and he resumed long-neglected activities with his wife and children. He felt like a valuable member of his family once more. The use of medical cannabis allowed Daniel and his family quality of life despite his back injury.

Q: Does cannabis use cause brain damage?

No claim that cannabis causes brain damage has ever been success-fully proven. In fact, all indications are that cannabis decreases the brain inflammation and subsequent cognitive losses associated with Alzheimer's disease (*O'Shaughnessy's*, Winter/Spring 2007, 11). Marilyn Bowman conducted psychological testing on chronic can-nabis users in Jamaica in 1972, and reported "no impairment of physiological, sensory, and perceptual-motor performance, tests of concept formation, abstracting ability, and cognitive style, and tests of memory" (Herer 2000, 114).

As Chris Conrad asked, "Why do the alcohol, tobacco, and phar-maceutical drug industries, all of which produce products that cause physical brain damage, contribute so much tax-deductible money to produce ads that trick people into thinking cannabis does?" (Conrad 1997, 143)

Q: Does smoking cannabis do more lung damage than tobacco?

Science has completely debunked this fear! The research findings of Donald Tashkin, MD, were featured on the front page of the Autumn 2005 issue of *O'Shaughnessy's*: "Marijuana smoking—even heavy long-term use—does not cause cancer of the lung, upper air-ways, or esophagus." Dr. Tashkin's study even indicated that can-nabis might provide a degree of protection against some lung cancers!

And what about tobacco? The American Lung Association has reported that approximately 430,000 Americans die from tobacco-related causes per year. Cigarette smoking causes one death out of every seven in the United States (Herer 2000, 112). And Vilma Hunt, a researcher at Harvard, discovered in 1964 that tobacco con-tains a *radioactive element!* I find it alarming that this information has not received more publicity. Dr. Edward Martell, a radiochemist working for the National Center for Atmospheric Research, stated, "There is enough polonium-210 in cigarettes to cause at least 95 percent of the lung cancer reported in smokers" (Herer 2000, 215).

The problem has been exacerbated by tobacco farmers' long-term use of phosphate fertilizers rich in uranium. Cannabis, on the other hand, requires no chemical fertilizers, herbicides, or pesticides to grow, and cannabis tars contain no radioactivity.

Q: Does cannabis use destroy or damage the immune system?

There is no valid scientific or medical evidence to support the fear that cannabis damages the immune system. On the contrary, a review of the history of cannabis medicine demonstrates the opposite. For example, cannabis has been used quite successfully to treat Crohn's disease. Although the cause of this inflammatory bowel disease is not yet understood, Jeffrey Hergenrather, MD, stated, "What can be said about [Crohn's disease] is that the immune system in the GI tract is overreactive, misguided, and destructive to the intestine. Components in cannabis are thought to exert some of their beneficial effects by interacting with cannabinoid receptors in the intestine. Cannabis-using Crohn's patients not only report significant relief of their symptoms, they are also able to reduce the amount of immunosuppressive medications that have been a mainstay of conventional treatment" (*O'Shaughnessy's,* Autumn 2005, 3).

Physicians who practice cannabis medicine consistently describe it as safe and nontoxic. A list of chronic conditions successfully treated by cannabis, compiled by Tod Mikuriya, MD, includes, "Autoimmune Disease 279.4" (*O'Shaughnessy's,* Autumn 2005, 2). The March 1999 report of the IOM states that extensive research has failed to demonstrate immune system damage from cannabis use (Herer 2000, 132).

(While I was doing the final edit on this book, I received e-mail from http://www.physorg.com/that so excited me I had to include the information! The article was titled, *"Cannabis could hold the key to ending multiple sclerosis misery."* According to this article, a research team of UK, European, Japanese, and U.S. scientists, led by David Baker, professor of neuroimmunology at Queen Mary, University of London, "found that doses of the active component within cannabis, tetrahydrocannabinol (THC), could significantly inhibit the development and severity of MS [multiple sclerosis]." It was already known that cannabis could relieve symptoms of multiple sclerosis and could slow the progression of disability, but the effect of cannabis on the underlying, immune aspects of the disease had not previously been investigated. Cannabis medications may help block the autoimmune response that triggers the development of multiple sclerosis. *That* is exciting news!)

Q: Will cannabis use during pregnancy cause fetal damage?

Women have historically used cannabis to treat nausea associated with pregnancy and to relieve pain and assist relaxation during childbirth without documented harm. Melanie Dreher, PhD, RN, conducted studies in Jamaica, and Dr. Peter Fried in Canada, that showed "minimal fetal effects" with cannabis use during pregnancy (*O'Shaughnessy's,* Spring 2006, 5). However, any substance should be used with great caution during pregnancy. This is an individual decision that I recommend be made in consultation with your personal physician, your obstetrician, your pediatrician, and your cannabis specialist.

Q: Does cannabis use cause other physical or mental problems?

Cannabis is one of the most harmless, yet beneficial, natural medicines in existence. As Jack Herer stated, "Some ten thousand studies have been done on cannabis, four thousand in the United States, and only about a dozen have shown any negative results and these have *never* been replicated" (Herer 2000, 43). In September 1998, after taking medical testimony for fifteen days, Francis Young, Administrative Law Judge for the DEA, stated, "Marijuana is one of the safest therapeutically-active substances known to man" (Herer 2000, 42). The evidence seems clear that the prohibition of medicinal cannabis and industrial hemp is not about protecting people—it is about protecting power and profits!

REFERENCES

Armentano, Paul. 2007. Emerging Clinical Applications of Cannabis. *O'Shaughnessy's, The Journal of Cannabis in Clinical Practice* (Winter/Spring): 11–15.

Clarke, Robert Connell. 1981. *Marijuana Botany: The Propagation and Breeding of Distinctive Cannabis.* Berkeley, California: And/Or Press, Inc.

Conrad, Chris. 1997. *Hemp For Health: The Medicinal and Nutritional Uses of Cannabis Sativa.* Rochester, Vermont: Healing Arts Press.

Dorland's Illustrated Medical Dictionary, Twenty-sixth Edition. Philadelphia: W.B. Saunders Company, 1985.

Frank, Mel. 1988. *Marijuana Grower's Insider's Guide.* Los Angeles, California: Red Eye Press.

Gardner, Fred. 2005. Dr. X's Talks of Special Interest. *O'Shaughnessy's, The Journal of Cannabis in Clinical Practice* (Autumn): 10 (items 5 and 9).

Gardner, Fred. 2007. Lab Studies by Cannabinoid Researchers Help Explain Clinical Reports of Efficacy. *O'Shaughnessy's, The Journal of Cannabis in Clinical Practice* (Winter/Spring): 9.

Gardner, Fred. 2005. Smoking Cannabis Does Not Cause Cancer of Lung or Upper Airways, Tashkin Finds; Data Suggest Possible Protective Effect. *O'Shaughnessy's, The Journal of Cannabis in Clinical Practice* (Autumn): 1, 9–10.

Gardner, Fred. 2006. Dreher Recounts Jamaican Study on Cannabis Use in Pregnancy. *O'Shaughnessy's, The Journal of Cannabis in Clinical Practice* (Spring): 5.

Herer, Jack. 2000. *The Emperor Wears No Clothes, Eleventh Edition.* Austin, Texas: AH HA Publishing.

Hergenrather, Jeffrey, MD. 2007. Medical Marijuana in California, 1996-2006. *O'Shaughnessy's, The Journal of Cannabis in Clinical Practice* (Winter/Spring): 1.

Hergenrather, Jeffrey, MD. 2005. Cannabis Alleviates Symptoms of Crohn's Disease. *O'Shaughnessy's, The Journal of Cannabis in Clinical Practice* (Autumn): 3.

Mikuriya, Tod, Jeffrey Hergenrather, Philip A. Denney, Frank H. Lucido, David Bearman, Claudia Jensen, Tom O'Connell, et al. 2007. Medical Marijuana in California, 1996-2006. *O'Shaughnessy's, The Journal of Cannabis in Clinical Practice* (Winter/Spring): 1, 4-8.

Mikuriya, Tod, MD. 2005. Chronic Conditions Treated with Cannabis. *O'Shaughnessy's, The Journal of Cannabis in Clinical Practice* (Autumn): 2.

O'Connell, Tom, MD. 2005. Implications of Early Cannabis Initiation. *O'Shaughnessy's, The Journal of Cannabis in Clinical Practice* (Autumn): 8.

O' Keefe, Katherine, and Mitch Earleywine. 2005. Use by Teens Declines in States With Medical Marijuana Laws. *O'Shaughnessy's, The Journal of Cannabis in Clinical Practice* (Autumn): 8.

Patients Out of Time. http://www.medicalcannabis.com/news.htm. *Marijuana Myths: Ten Most Common Concerns About Cannabis.*

Physorg: Science: Physics: Tech: Nano: News. http://www.physorg. com/. *Cannabis could hold the key to ending multiple sclerosis misery.*

PART II

Growing Cannabis

Before you begin reading this, be aware that there are many books available on growing cannabis that go into great depth and detail and are very scientific and professional, with lots of graphs, charts, and numbers. Some are listed in my references. I recommend this type of book if you desire a more technical approach to growing, or if you need information on indoor or hydroponic gardening. On the other hand, if that much information just leaves you confused, check out the following suggestions and techniques for growing cannabis outdoors in a home garden situation.

My techniques have evolved over time from a combination of study of just such books as I discussed above, and from thirty-five years of gardening experience. Much of what I know I learned from my mother and grandmothers. Our home in the Sierra Nevada Mountains is surrounded by organic flower gardens. If you find the very complex books confusing, this should be a good starting place.

You can grow excellent medicinal cannabis without a PhD, I promise you.

Chapter Two

Beginnings

Starting from Seed

Growing cannabis from seed has some advantages and some disadvantages. Plants started from seed generally grow strong and healthy. They tend to mature two to three weeks earlier than clones of the same strain. This can be an important consideration if your growing season is short. And it's the only way to custom breed your own varieties.

On the other hand, when you grow from seed, potency varies, and it is my experience that while you may end up with an outstanding individual or two, most of your females will produce mediocre medicine. That's because most of us aren't starting hundreds to thousands of seeds to obtain the numbers that would yield several excellent females. With smaller numbers, plant potency is largely a matter of luck.

Basically, I use seed when that is the only way to obtain a desired variety, or when I have crossbred some seed of my own that I want to test. My ultimate goal is always to end up with a high-quality female from which to produce clones in the future.

Start your seed indoors, about three months before your last frost and intended planting date. If you don't know your gardening zone or the dates of first and last frosts, contact your local county extension agent, consult a gardening book (such as *Sunset Western Garden Book*), or ask other local gardeners when the first and last frosts usually occur. Starting this early gives you time to determine the gender of your seedlings prior to planting, allowing you to set only females out in the garden, instead of wasting space on male plants.

Storing Seed

Cannabis seed is best preserved by being stored in the refrigerator or freezer in a dark, airtight container, such as a labeled black film canister. Place the canister inside a sealed plastic bag. Make sure that the stored seed is dry and free of vegetative material. I have successfully kept seed viable this way for several years.

Materials

Seeds
Small glass jar(s)
Sterile organic potting soil (can add extra vermiculite and/or perlite)
Seed-starting heat mat large enough to hold all the pots of seed you will start (available through garden catalogs and hydroponics stores)
Four-by-four-inch plastic nursery pots
Tray(s) to catch water draining from the pots
Fluorescent grow light or a double fluorescent fixture with warm and cool tubes, with a baffle and a way to mount the light above the plants
Timer for the light
Plant labels (white plastic excellent)
Indelible marker

Instructions

Bring your seed to room temperature. Select plump, fully colored, undamaged seeds. I test them by gently squeezing each seed between my thumb and forefinger. If the seed does not collapse, it is usually viable. Larger seeds are better, as very small seeds often reflect a wild hemp ancestry. Place the seeds into labeled glass jars, and cover with tepid water overnight.

The next day, drain the seeds, and set out the necessary number of four-by-four-inch pots for the seeds you will plant. If the seeds are fresh, you can probably plant one seed per pot. If they're older, I plant up to four seeds in each pot to ensure that at least one comes up. (Of course, I have had them all sprout when I've done this!) Fill the pots with damp, not soggy, sterile potting soil, and place them in their trays so the water has somewhere to drain when you water them. Always use tepid water. You can add extra vermiculite or perlite to your potting soil if you wish. Vermiculite is designed to retain water, and perlite holds oxygen, both vital components for growth. Both these amendments will increase the soil's drainage.

Label each pot before you plant the seeds. That way, you can't mix anything up or forget in which pot you planted which seeds. I use white plastic plant labels that follow each plant throughout its life cycle. Do not label by the row, telling yourself you'll remember—you won't. You'll forget and move some plants out of their row, trust me. This is the only way I've found not to mix up my plants.

By now you should have pots lined up, filled with damp potting soil and sitting in their catch trays. They should be labeled and ready to be planted.

Make a depression in the soil in each pot about the depth of a pencil eraser (one-quarter inch), which is what I use. If you're planting more than one seed per pot, space your holes around the middle of the pot. You'll eventually leave only one plant in the pot, and you want it close to the middle, not stuck off in a corner. Carefully drop a seed into each hole, making sure you're planting the right seed in the right pot. Cover the seeds, patting the soil down gently. Sprinkle with tepid water to eliminate air pockets. After the pots have finished draining, empty the catch trays. It is important that pots never sit in standing water, which prevents the soil and roots from exchanging oxygen.

Set the pots, in their tray, on top of an appropriately-sized heat mat. The heat mat will stay on all the time. Bottom heat is absolutely essential. You can purchase seed-starting heat mats through garden catalogs, hydroponics centers, and some nurseries.

(*Warning:* carefully protect any surface you place the mat on. I had a heat mat buckle the surface of a vinyl floor, even though I had a folded towel under it.)

The plants don't need any light at all until they sprout, but then they need light immediately, so rig it and get it ready now. There are several ways to hang lights. You can purchase indoor growing systems that are designed to suspend a grow light above plants. Hydroponics stores should have a good selection of this type of setup, as do many garden catalogs. These work and are quick and easy but can be costly and only hold a limited number of plants. If your needs are small and you can afford it, a system like this is a good way for you to go. Alternatively, you can suspend a two- or four-foot fluorescent fixture from the ceiling or from a wooden or metal framework. Use small chains that you can adjust up or down to hang the fixture. Either use an actual grow light, or use a double fixture, and fill it with one warm and one cool tube to give the plants the spectrum of light they need.

The light should be positioned right above the tops of the pots. Once the seeds sprout and start growing, keep the light only one to two inches above the tops of the plants, and adjust it as they grow. If the light is kept too high, the seedlings will grow long and leggy and will be unable to support themselves: they'll flop over. If some plants grow taller than others, line them up by height, and slant the light. (If you are using a metal halide or high pressure sodium lamp, you will keep it eighteen inches to three feet above the plants and will still need to watch that tender young seedlings don't fry. Follow manufacturer's directions.)

While you're waiting for your seeds to sprout, keep the soil surface damp, but not soggy. Wetting the surface with a spray bottle of tepid water is best, as this does not disturb the seeds.

Growing Seedlings

Once the seeds sprout, which usually takes anywhere from a few days to two weeks, depending upon their age and condition, keep them on eighteen hours of light per day for at least one month. The plants will need to have developed a minimum of four sets of leaves before you determine their gender or sex them.

Water when the surface of the soil is dry to approximately one-half inch. Two weeks after sprouting, begin fertilizing with a liquid organic fertilizer (such as fish fertilizer or Omega 6-6-6) that you mix with kelp, following package directions. I purchase my organic products from Peaceful Valley Farm & Garden Supply in Grass Valley, California. They carry the highest-quality cold-processed liquid kelp (Algamin) I have ever found, they support organic practices and products, and they're willing to take orders by phone and ship them to your door. (Another good nursery in California that specializes in organic growing is The Golden Gecko, in Garden Valley, California.)

The Omega line of fertilizers is a product of microbial fermentation that stimulates soil life and depresses elements that suppress seed germination. Although they are primarily intended as starter fertilizers, I use them with excellent results throughout the plants' life cycle. (Contact information for Peaceful Valley Farm & Garden Supply: 888-784-1722 or http://www.GrowOrganic.com/.)

If you planted multiple seeds per pot and more than one seed in a pot sprouts, keep the healthiest seedling, and either cut the rest of the seedlings in the pot off at the base, so as not to disturb the roots of the one you leave, or transplant them into pots in which no seeds sprouted. *Do not* pull them up. (Note that the tallest seedling is not necessarily the healthiest.) You can transplant seedlings as soon as they've fully opened their first set of little round leaves (cotyledons), but do so only if the seedling is far enough from the others to insert a teaspoon into the soil between it and any other sprout. To transplant, make a hole for the root ball in the soil of the pot to which you will transplant. Then insert a teaspoon into the soil beside the seedling you wish to move, burying the bowl of the spoon to its neck, and carefully lift the tiny plant out, with the roots nestled within a small wedge of soil. Slide the intact soil wedge off the tip of the spoon and into the hole you prepared, guiding it with your fingers. Firm the soil gently and water. Go back to the other pot, and smooth and firm the soil around the seedling you left behind. If you need to add soil, use the soil you removed from the pot into which you transplanted. Water them both to eliminate air pockets. Let the surface of the soil dry before watering again to prevent damping off or stem rot.

When your plants are one month old and have at least four sets of true leaves (cotyledons don't count as true leaves), you can sex them. Gender differentiation in cannabis is triggered by a decrease in the photoperiod. Cut your lights down to twelve hours per day, and keep the plants completely in the dark for the other twelve hours. Room light will interrupt the cycle of dark and light and prevent gender differentiation.

After about two weeks of twelve hours of light per day, the plants will start forming immature buds. Males will probably show first. Early flowers occur near the top of the plant, where a leaf joins the stem. You'll find a tiny ball nestled there with no stigma (or pistil) protruding out of it if it's a male. (See illustration.) Watch it and wait if you're unsure. If it starts making more little balls around the first, without stigmas, you definitely have a male. (I usually wait for this to happen, because females don't always have stigmas at first. This way, I'm sure of the correct gender.) Discard or compost your males. A female blooms in the same place, but its ball is a little more oval and has one or two tiny white stigmas sticking out of it. (See illustration.) Use of a magnifying glass can help. The majority of your plants will sex within the same one to two week period of time. It has been my experience that plants that take longer than this to differentiate gender initially show a female sex, then they turn hermaphroditic later in the season, producing male blossoms beside the female buds and seeding my whole crop if I don't catch them out. I cull any plants that have not differentiated gender within about two weeks of the date the first plant showed its sex.

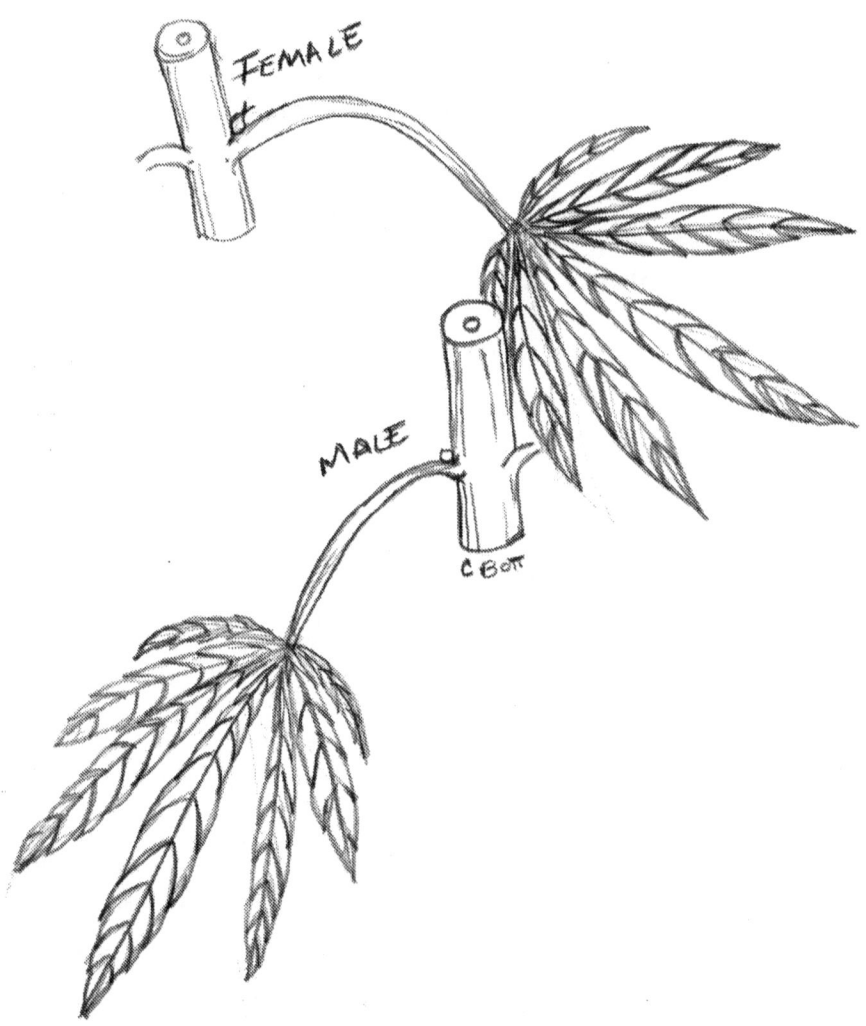

Depiction of immature male and female buds.

Once you've sexed out your females, you can plant them right into the garden if the weather allows. (Remember to harden them off prior to planting outside. Instructions for this can be found under chapter three, in the part on planting and training.) If you still need to hold them until frost danger is past, the ground is warm, and the days are long enough, move them into one-gallon nursery pots. Continue feeding as before. Keep the plants on a heat mat until you're ready to harden them off. Water when the soil is dry down to one inch in these larger pots. Increase the light cycle back to eighteen hours per day. Increased light will cause the females to revert to vegetative growth, usually manifested by starting all over again with a one-lobed leaf.

If the weather is clement enough to allow you to set the plants outside during the day, this is very good for them and helps prevent disease. Set them out, initially, in full sun, but watch them. Move any plants that wilt into the shade for a couple of days, and then move them back out into full sun and try again. This also helps harden off the young plants. (If you are doing this, you will only have the plants on a heat mat during the night, when they're inside.)

Starting from Clones

Clones are vegetative cuttings that have been taken from a mature female and have been rooted. Using clones has several advantages over starting plants from seed. Clones taken from the same mother plant are genetically identical; you're growing a known quantity. All the plants will be female. Plants of the same variety will grow the same and be equally potent, assuming consistent growing conditions.

The simplest way to obtain clones is to buy or trade for them, if you can find them. They can be purchased from dispensaries and cooperatives or from individual growers, and usually cost about ten dollars per plant. Purchasing clones, however, will limit the varieties available to you, the quality of the plants will vary, and you may not know for sure that the plants were raised organically. You will also be unable to assure yourself of a supply of clones each year. Alternatively, you can make your own clones, guaranteeing a self-sufficient supply from year to year and introducing the specific varieties you want. This is also a good way to preserve a special favorite, highly medicinal female, or specialized local variety.

Making your own Clones

In order to have clones to plant in spring, you need to start them in late summer of the previous year, if you are cloning outside stock. If you started several females of the same variety from seed and don't know which will turn out to be best, take clones from them all. After harvest, evaluate the cannabis from each female and then keep the clone of the most medicinal (if any are worth saving). Discard or compost the rest. You now have your high-quality mother.

Materials

Rockwool cubes, small (hydroponics stores)
Very sharp shears or a straight-edge razor (Hydroponics stores sell little scissors designed for this type of cutting and trimming.)
Rooting compound, gel, or liquid (hydroponics stores—*not* the powder from the grocery store)
Heat mat
Drainage trays
Perlite
Screens (See instructions below.)
Jars of water to hold cut stems, labeled
Jar of water for final cut
Fluorescent lights as for seedlings (*Do not* use metal halide or sodium vapor lamps.)

Timer
Plant labels
Indelible marker

Instructions

First, prepare your trays. I use the same trays for this that I use to catch water when growing seedlings; I just make sure I wash them before I use them. Put perlite into a tray to at least one inch. (Remember: perlite retains oxygen, vital for root formation.) Over this, put some type of larger plastic mesh screen that roots from the clones can grow through without becoming entangled (at least one-fourth inch mesh). I use garden pruning shears to cut out the plastic mesh bottoms of nursery flats for my screening. You can wash and reuse them for years, and the mesh is big enough not to trap the growing roots; you just have to work them out of it carefully.

Set the number of rockwool cubes you will use in a tray or bowl that will hold water, and dampen them thoroughly with tepid water. Prepare your labels. You will insert a plastic label into each cube after planting in it.

Before the plants growing outside are in full bloom, around the end of July or early August in Northern California, take cuttings from the females you want to preserve. Pick small, lower, or middle branches that aren't going to give you much bud anyway. Older, woody stems root better than soft, new, green growth. You will ideally choose stems that are no bigger around than a pencil, yet not microscopic. Cut your chosen stems as you would for a bouquet, cutting them longer than you will actually need. Put them into a labeled jar of water and take them into the house to finish.

Remove a stem from a jar. Strip all the leaves off below the top one or two sets of leaves. Remove very large leaves or trim them; they will take too much energy from the plant while it's trying to root.

Pick a leaf node (a slightly raised spot where leaves were growing) at least four nodes down from the top. Holding the stem underwater in the cutting jar, make a slanting cut just below the chosen leaf node. (See illustration.) Slanting the cut allows more surface area for rooting. Dip your cutting into your rooting compound, following package directions, and insert it carefully into the hole that's already in the top of the rockwool cube, stopping when you feel resistance. Be careful not to damage or bend the stem, which should not go all the way through the cube. Stick the label into a spare corner of the cube and set the cube on the screen placed over perlite. Continue this procedure for the rest of your cuttings. Water them all again with tepid water until the level of the water is just below the top of the perlite. Finish off by spraying the foliage with tepid water, wetting the undersides of the leaves as well as the tops.

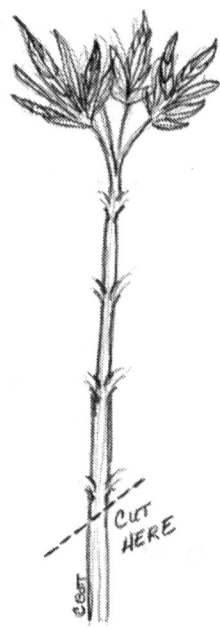

This shows where and how to make the final cut for a clone.

Set the tray of cuttings on a heat mat, which will stay on all the time. Fluorescent lights should be kept four to six inches from the tops of the plants and should be on from eighteen to twenty-four hours per day. (Clones root best under fluorescent lights.) I feel that having some dark period is more natural for the plants, so I use eighteen hours instead of twenty-four hours.

Water the cubes with tepid water when they start to dry out and lighten in color. Don't keep them soaked all the time, or your stems will rot. Spray the clones with water at least once a day; more often is much better. I spray mine five to ten times a day. Be sure to wet the undersides of the leaves. After the first two or three days, spray with a half-strength liquid organic fertilizer designed to encourage vegetative growth, mixed with half-strength liquid kelp. (See the seed starting part for more details regarding fertilizer.) Do this once per week, and use plain, tepid water in between. Your clones will start showing roots anywhere from two to six weeks, sometimes sooner, depending upon the strain, the health of the clone, and the growing conditions.

Potting Clones

Materials

One-gallon nursery pots (four-by-four-inch pots are okay if the plants will not be in them longer than one month.)
Potting soil
Mycorrhizae inoculant (Optional: this is a mix of soil organisms found at garden centers, nurseries, and in garden catalogs.)
Drainage trays
Heat mat
Grow light (High pressure sodium or metal halide lamps work best but cost a lot to buy and to run; you can make do with fluorescent

tubes, especially with the addition of some daylight through a window. This works and saves literally hundreds of dollars a month while your plants are inside.)

Instructions

When you lift a clone and find a healthy ball of roots at least the size of a walnut protruding from the rockwool, or when you try to lift the clone and find it firmly anchored into the rockwool, it's ready to plant. To lift the clone, work the roots gently and carefully out of the perlite and through the plastic screen. Don't worry about the perlite left clinging to the roots.

Fill the number of pots you are going to use with damp potting soil, tamping it down gently, and set them out in their tray. Water lightly to settle the soil, and add more soil if you need to. Remember to leave enough room to water the plants later without the pots overflowing. Using your finger, make a hole in the soil a bit bigger and deeper than the roots of the plant. Put mycorrhizae inoculant, if you are using it, in the bottom of the hole, following package directions. Set the rooted rockwool cube into that hole, with just the top of the cube sticking out of the soil; this will help oxygen flow through the roots. Using your finger as needed, work the roots down into the hole. Carefully and gently firm the soil around the cube and roots. Irrigate with tepid water to eliminate any air pockets. Take the label out of the rockwool, and insert it in the soil at the edge of the pot.

Once your rooted clones are all planted, set the tray on a heat mat, and place them under eighteen hours of light a day, just as described in the seed starting part. The heat mat will stay on as long as the plants are inside. (If you leave newly planted clones in cold soil, their roots are likely to shrivel and disappear, killing the plant.) The clones will be rooted into the pots within a couple of weeks. At this point, if you've taken plants in summer for the following year, just hold them indoors under lights and on a heat mat over winter, feeding and watering as previously instructed. You can keep them in gallon pots all winter, but they're happier in three-gallon pots, if you have the room.

In February or March, I start new clones for that year's planting, using the plants I held over winter as mothers. The new clones can be planted into four-by-four-inch pots, because they'll soon be set out into the garden, although I prefer to use gallon pots. By this time, the mothers will have been used up and composted, or discarded if there is disease on their leaves.

(*Warning:* always watch indoor plants for diseases and pests. Spider mites are especially ubiquitous where it is warm and dry, and fungal diseases will show up if the environment is damp and cool. Poor air circulation almost always causes difficulties. If you discover a problem, refer to the part on pests and diseases in chapter three. The same solutions work inside or outside. If air circulation is a problem, run a fan.)

Chapter Three

Growing Outdoors

Selecting and Preparing the Site

Select an accessible garden site in full sun. This translates to no less than six to eight hours of direct sun per day; more is definitely better. I situate my plants in the garden with everything else, mixing them right in with the flowers, herbs, and berries, but I do attempt to keep them in inconspicuous locations. I believe this to be purely prudent. (Some growers routinely plant among their tomatoes, and this also works well.)

You need to space your plants a minimum of three feet apart, and that spacing will leave them crowded at the end of the season. If you can plant farther apart, they will be happier and healthier, and it will be easier for you to work among them. Eight feet apart is not extravagant. A spot that is protected from the wind is best.

Ideally, you should rotate sites, not planting in the same spot year after year. However, most of us can't do that due to space limitations. When you use the same spot every year, you've depleted the soil in that site at the end of each growing season. You will need to thoroughly amend the soil the next year before planting again. Also, be sure to clean the area up thoroughly in the fall to prevent diseases and insects from carrying over winter to plague you the next year.

After fall cleanup, mulch the bare soil with leaves, pine needles, straw, or herbicide, and pesticide-free grass clippings, piling the mulch at least six inches deep. This protects the soil structure and microorganisms throughout winter and provides some nutrients from decomposition in the spring. Mulching also keeps weeds down. Pull the mulch back from the planting spots once the worst storms of spring are past to allow the soil to dry and warm up.

It is my experience that you'll be fine if you follow these basic precautions.

Preparing the Soil

Cannabis needs very good drainage; plan on amending your soil. Amend the soil in each planting spot, rather than in the whole bed—why fix soil in pathways?

To begin, dig an area a minimum of four square feet, digging down through any hardpan and piling the soil you dig out beside the hole. Every year, dig the hole a little bigger and deeper than the year before, so drainage keeps improving.

Before you refill the hole you dug and amend the soil, you need to test the drainage of the spot; do this every year. Testing drainage will be necessary even if you intend to use drip irrigation. Fill the hole with water. Watch to be sure the spot drains fairly quickly; the level of the water should visibly recede. If it drains slowly, you'll need to dig deeper. If the hole won't drain at all and is just sitting there filled with muddy water, try driving a metal pole, such as a piece of rebar, through the bottom of the planting hole in several spots to improve drainage. Repeat these procedures until the hole drains well. (I had to dig a boulder out of a spot once before it would drain.)

Once you have good drainage, you're ready to fill up the hole and amend the soil. Wait until any remaining water has completely drained from the hole. Then refill it by layering the soil you dug out with homemade (or purchased) compost, beginning and ending with compost. You won't use up all the soil you dug out; use the leftovers to build a raised rim around the planting hole, creating a well to hold water. This is especially necessary if you plan to water by hand from a hose, your summers are extremely hot and dry, your planting area is exposed to winds, you are planting on a slope, or if your soil is sandy and dries out quickly.

If you don't make your own compost, but want to, I have provided directions. Otherwise, I suggest purchasing high-quality organic compost. It's often possible to buy something like mushroom compost or other organic mixtures in bulk from garden centers, nurseries, or establishments that sell landscape materials. (For example, my friend, Judy, just bought a whole truckload of rice hulls mixed with turkey manure.) Just make sure you don't buy compost that is primarily bark or other wood products. This will have little nutrition and may deplete the soil of nitrogen if the wood is not completely decomposed.

Other optional soil amendments include such things as rice hulls to improve soil drainage and texture and composted (decomposed) manures for nutrition. The best manures for our area of Northern California are bird, dairy, and sheep. It is better to avoid the use of steer and horse manures no matter where you live; they often contain high levels of salts and pesticides.

(*Never* apply raw manure just before planting; compost it first. Raw manure will burn your plants. If you want to apply raw manure to your garden, you must do so the fall before, so that it has all winter and spring to break down. Spread the manure no more than one inch deep if you are applying it raw to decompose on the site. Thoroughly mix the decomposed manure into the top twelve to eighteen inches of soil as soon as the ground can be worked the next spring.)

Mix a good, organic, granular fertilizer into the top twelve to eighteen inches of soil in each hole you prepared. I buy Sierra Foothill Fertilizer Mix with added nitrogen from Peaceful Valley Farm & Garden Supply (888-784-1722; http://www.GrowOrganic.com/), and mix about two cups into each planting spot. This organic, slow-release fertilizer has been formulated especially for the acidic, lean soils of the Northern California foothills. If you live elsewhere, with completely different soil, seek out a similar establishment in your geographical area. Alternatively, Foxfarm is another good organic brand to use that is more commonly available. Follow product directions.

(It's my experience that organic practices and the regular and consistent use of homemade compost automatically keep the soil in balance. However, you can always have your soil tested, although I've never done this in all the years I've gardened. If you choose to test the soil, contact your county extension agent for more information as to how to go about it. Then amend your soil accordingly, per the results of the soil survey.)

Making Your Own Compost

(*Warning:* use homemade compost outside, only! Never use any soil or amendment indoors that is not sterile. You will introduce pests and diseases that inside plants cannot deal with and that you will have a great deal of trouble eliminating.)

Making your own compost has several advantages. Above all, it's free, and you can make as much as you need. It provides nutrients and is an excellent soil amendment, promoting good drainage and healthy soil structure. Composting creates a venue for disposing of plant matter and food waste that would otherwise be burned or discarded, contributing to air pollution or taking up unnecessary room in landfills and dumps and luring wildlife into areas where they are in danger of injury or poisoning. Compost is an intricate and indispensable component of any form of organic gardening, which is not just about the things you *don't* do or *don't* use. The heart of organic gardening lies in what you *do* and involves actively living on and working the land in ways that encourage life, leaving the earth better, healthier, and more balanced. (Healthy gardens have bugs, birds, and bees, not to mention lizards, frogs, and snakes.) Finally, in my experience, homemade compost provides an array of nutrients, micronutrients, and soil microorganisms that is unique to the particular garden or area in which that compost was created. You can't buy this type of specialized food anywhere.

First, some general rules for composting: do not compost meat or dairy products, although eggshells are wonderful. Do not use any grass or other clippings that have been treated with herbicides or pesticides. And *never* compost any diseased or insect-infested foliage or other plant material. (Don't compost anything at all from roses, iris, or peonies.) You will introduce diseases and pests that you will never get rid of. Also, do not compost any plant that is seeded, unless you don't mind the seeds sprouting around your garden where you use the compost. Most homemade compost does not get hot enough to destroy all seeds. (In other words, I do not put weeds that are seeded into my compost, but I *do* put in dried up Sweet Alyssum plants, because I like them to spread.) Do not compost items such as office paper or bills; you can introduce high levels of toxic metals like lead. And *never* compost waste from household pets or people!

Do, however, compost used coffee grounds, tea bags, and loose tea. Leaving them in their paper filters is fine, especially if the filters are unbleached. You can sometimes arrange to pick such materials up in bulk from a local tea or coffee shop. They add nitrogen to your compost. It's also okay to peel and cut vegetables and fruits onto a paper towel, then gather the whole mess up in the towel and compost it. This has never caused me a problem, and the paper towel breaks right down.

If you live in a city or a suburban neighborhood with yards and houses close together, probably the best way to make compost is to purchase one of the tumblers or drum compost makers that are available through garden centers and catalogs. Follow the manufacturer's directions. This is a good solution for limited space and will avoid any problems with odor or unsightly piles. Units designed to compost indoors with earthworms are useful when all you have to put into compost is food waste. I've seen these in garden catalogs. They are said to be ideal for apartment dwellers.

If you have a large yard or live in the country, you can build your own compost pile. The simplest is just a layered pile of garden debris and food waste. You can leave the pile uncontained; you can circle it with chicken wire or fencing; or you can construct a simple compost bin out of wood or concrete blocks. My husband, Terry, cemented concrete blocks together to construct a two bin, open compost. The concrete walls absorb heat and keep the piles contained. Two bins allow me to keep finished compost in one bin, while continuing to actively compost in the other.

A compost pile requires sunlight, oxygen, and water to work. Locate your pile in as full a sun as possible. Build it up by layering what I term "green stuff" and "brown stuff." In other words, alternate layers of items like coffee grounds, fresh animal manures, food waste, grass clippings, and green plant debris with layers of dry leaves, pine needles, dry plant debris, and even clothes dryer lint. Make sure nothing is diseased or seeded. Carefully bury food waste in the pile to avoid attracting animals. You should add a shovel of soil occasionally. Tossing in a handful of organic granular fertilizer two or three times during the growing season doesn't hurt either. These things keep the level of microorganisms high and give the compost plenty to feed on.

Be aware that fresh animal manures may introduce weed seeds to your compost. Since I have no farm animals, I purchase one-cubic-foot bags of weed-free organic chicken manure and layer that into my compost pile throughout the growing season. I use three to five bags per year.

Oxygen is usually provided by regularly turning over your compost pile with a pitchfork or by poking holes in it with a specialized aerating tool. This is a lot of hard work! Instead, I layer small branches, sticks, and sturdier flower stalks into my pile during the season. They decompose more slowly than everything else and create air pockets throughout the compost that supply necessary oxygen.

This allows me to turn my pile only two times a year, in spring and fall, when I use up the current batch of finished compost and fork the working batch over into the bin I just emptied. I take the opportunity while I do that to add amendments, and I make sure the pile is thoroughly layered. I produce two large batches of compost each year this way.

If your summers are dry, water your compost pile as often as needed to keep it damp and working but not saturated and soggy. This works out to once or twice a week during the growing season for me. I just put a sprinkler on top of the pile, set a timer for half an hour, and go back to whatever I was doing at the time.

A pile of compost usually stops working during below-freezing weather, but just keep adding material to it as you have need (although you probably won't be able to bury food scraps). The freezing actually helps. Your compost will go to work with a vengeance as soon as the weather warms up in spring and the pile thaws. You'll have beautiful, finished compost in no time!

Planting and Training

Wait until after the last frost date in your area to plant your cannabis, which is a frost-tender annual. If you do not know your gardening zone or first and last frost dates, contact your local county extension agent, or consult a gardening book or catalog that shows garden zones, such as *Sunset Western Garden Book*. You can also ask other local gardeners when the first and last frosts usually occur.

Be sure you're working with plants that have been hardened off if they were previously growing indoors. This means that you have given the plants a chance to get used to outside conditions and temperatures before planting them out. To harden off your indoor seedlings or clones, set them outside during the day for four or five days, bringing them in at night. (This is the only time you can choose *not* to put them back on a heat mat.) Start them off in partial shade, and move them into full sun after a couple of days. Watch carefully at first to be sure they don't wilt. If they do, move them back into the shade for another couple of days, and try again. Also, be sure the sun is not making the pots so hot that the roots cook; black nursery pots are notorious for this. If the outsides of the pots feel hot, wrap white paper or cloth (such as an old sheet) around the pots, or shade them in some other way. Just avoid shading the plants themselves. After the plants have withstood full sun for a couple of days, leave them out all day and all night for another three or four days. They should be ready to sit out with minimal transplant shock after this treatment. Be sure to keep them well watered when they first encounter the strength of the full sun.

To plant, scoop or dig a hole in the prepared soil that is approximately twice as large as the plant's root ball. Fill the hole once with water, and let it thoroughly drain. Add mycorrhizae inoculant to the spot if you are using it. Take care that the plants you are going to set out have been well watered. Gently tap or strike the bottom of the plant pot to loosen the root ball. Then slide the plant out of its pot, catching the top of the root ball flat in the palm of your other hand where the stem meets the soil. Let the base of the stem slip between your index and second fingers. Do not tug or pull on the stem or carry the plant by its stem.

Turn the plant upright, and plant the root ball so that the plant is growing at approximately the same level as it was in its pot. Gently firm the soil around the plant with your hands, and water thoroughly. (*Do not* stomp the soil around the plant with your foot!) For the initial watering, fill up the well around the plant three times with water, letting it drain completely between fillings. (Don't worry if drainage time slows by the third time.) Do not direct the stream of water onto the plant. Be sure to set out the plant label.

Mulch around each plant to help retain water, suppress weeds, and shade the soil. Use the same types of materials as I recommended using for mulching the site in the fall, again piling your mulch at least six inches deep. Be careful to keep the mulch a minimum of twelve inches away from the stem of the cannabis plant. Mulching right up to the stem can introduce disease and cause rot. (If you've created wells around your plants, mulch to the rims of the wells, but not inside them.)

Your plants should be fine in full sun right away if they were properly hardened off, but sometimes a plant wilts anyway. If a plant does look wilted, shade it from the sun for a few days, and keep it well watered. I use light shade cloth, held off the plant with sticks and held down along the edge with rocks or soil, or an old, perforated laundry basket for this. Weight the laundry basket down so it doesn't blow away. The plant should recover quickly once you provide shade and should be able to tolerate full sun within a week.

As your plants start to really take off, you will need to decide whether or not you are going to cut them back (top them) or let them grow unmolested. There are advantages and disadvantages to both methods. Some growers believe that plants are more stable in storms and don't fall over as much when they have kept their natural Christmas tree shape. They also like to harvest the large, top cola (bud) that forms. On the other hand, not topping the plants reduces the overall harvest, and the grower cannot control how tall his or her plants become. This can be a security risk.

Topping the plants increases the total amount of medicine you harvest by spreading colas across the whole upper surface of the plant, although the buds will probably individually be a bit smaller. (When a plant is cut back, it develops several main stems in place of the solitary leader it had before.) Topping also allows you to control the ultimate height of the plant. The disadvantage of topping is that the plants may not stand up as well to wind and rain because they are top heavy. Nevertheless, I top my plants, cutting them back one to three times per season. I believe that the current, somewhat muddied legal status of medical cannabis calls for controlling plant size, and I like to increase the harvest from each plant, allowing me to grow fewer plants overall. I am prepared to support the plants by staking or caging them.

If you are going to cut your cannabis plants back, wait until they have really started growing and are sprouting up fast and becoming leggy. When they are ready, pick the height you want for the plant at that time, then cut it back to that height, making a slanted cut just above a pair of leaves. Be careful to leave at least four sets of leaves on the plant. (You slant the cut to allow water and other liquids to run off, instead of puddle on the end of the cut and rot the stem.) You will probably not need to top your cannabis until the plants have been in the ground for at least one month. You will have to repeat the cutting only if part of a plant is beginning to shoot up rapidly and outgrow everything else, or if a plant is becoming so tall it is a security risk. One topping is often enough. *Do not* cut a plant back that is within two weeks of blooming.

Another way to limit plant height and increase harvest is to espalier the plant. To do this, select several main branches, and pull them out horizontally; secure them against a fence or trellis, or tie them off to a ground stake. (You can even stake them right along the ground, just put layers of newspaper, heavy cardboard, or some other ground cover that water will pass through beneath each branch to keep it from drawing moisture and rotting. *Do not* use plastic; water will puddle on it.) Prune away small, vertical, or competing growth. Buds will form along the entire length of each branch, instead of just at the end.

Be aware that this method is labor intensive. The branches will continually turn back up to the light as they grow, and you will need to keep tying them down as they lengthen. Plus, you will have to tie down and train new branches as they form. This becomes so time consuming as the season progresses, it is my opinion that espaliering is primarily useful where very careful security is required, or where space is extremely limited. Under those conditions, this method can be quite effective.

Feeding

Remember that you mixed organic granular fertilizer and compost into the soil at planting; however, cannabis is a heavy feeder, like corn. After your plants have been in the ground two weeks to one month and are displaying healthy new growth, start supplementary feedings. Foliar feed (spray the leaves, paying special attention to the leaf undersides) per product directions, using an organic liquid fertilizer that you mix with liquid kelp. Plants absorb nutrients through their leaves, as well as their roots. Spray once every one to two weeks. (I usually spray once every two weeks, but sometimes the plants start looking a little pale during the height of summer, when they are growing very rapidly. That's when I increase supplementary feedings to once a week, and make very sure they're getting enough water. I again use Omega 6-6-6 fertilizer mixed with kelp.)

Cannabis needs a fairly balanced supply of the three major nutrients—nitrogen, phosphorus, and potassium—during vegetative growth. (The three numbers on a bag or package of fertilizer represent those nutrients, in that order. Omega 6-6-6 and 1-5-5 are good examples of this.) Nitrogen helps your plants stay green and healthy, and it promotes vegetative growth. Phosphorus helps them bloom and bud well. Potassium makes strong roots and stems. You can use a fertilizer that has a higher percentage of nitrogen (for example, 10-6-6) during vegetative growth. This is often the case when using fish fertilizers. As long as you are using an organic fertilizer that has all three nutrients present and are following product directions, a higher percentage of nitrogen during this period of rapid growth is fine.

Once the days have shortened, and the plants begin blooming, switch to a fertilizer designed to promote bloom, such as Omega 1-5-5 or Foxfarm Big Bud. High levels of nitrogen during the blooming period will interfere with bud development by encouraging vegetative growth. You also need to switch from feeding by foliar spraying to watering the soil around the plant (soil douche), to avoid wetting the developing buds. More phosphorus in relation to potassium during the blooming period helps bud formation. To accomplish this, I mix some high-phosphorus seabird guano (1-10-0) that I order from Peaceful Valley Farm & Garden Supply with Omega 1-5-5 and kelp. I water the plants with it once every one to two weeks, depending upon the condition of the plants, using about one gallon of mixture per plant. (Keep stirring the liquid mixture up as you work.)

Kelp supplies necessary micronutrients and helps the plants resist disease. I use it throughout the life of the plant. I purchase cold-processed liquid kelp (Algamin) from Peaceful Valley Farm & Garden Supply (888-784-1722; http://www.GrowOrganic.com/). They carry the highest-quality kelp I have encountered.

Discontinue all supplementary feeding at least two weeks prior to harvest to allow any excess nutrients to flush from the plant tissues. Keep the plants well watered.

Watering

Cannabis needs to be watered deeply and thoroughly and then allowed to dry a bit before being watered again. Don't keep it soggy. If the surface of the soil never dries out, you'll have disease and insect problems, and the roots will be stunted. To test for watering needs, stick your finger in the soil or dig into it with a garden trowel one to three feet from the base of the plant, depending upon the size of the plant's canopy. The more area the canopy covers, the farther away from the stem you test. Water when the soil is dry down to the depth of your finger, or three to four inches. Don't wet the foliage when you water. If you are hand watering with a hose, you will want to fill up the well around each plant two to three times. Check after the water drains to see how deeply it penetrated.

I use drip irrigation, running it for three hours at a time, usually once every two to three days during the summer. We place twenty drip emitters around each plant. The emitters release one-half gallon of water per hour at thirty pounds per square inch, delivering ten gallons an hour, or thirty gallons over three hours. Terry determined how much water we needed by giving the plants what he thought was adequate moisture and then digging into the soil beside them to see how deeply the water had penetrated. He kept adding watering time (or emitters) until the soil surrounding each plant was wet down to at least twelve to eighteen inches immediately after completing the irrigation. To determine the required frequency of irrigation, Terry repeated the digging and checking every day until water was again necessary.

Watch carefully and be ready to meet increasing needs for water during the height of summer, when days are hot and dry and plants are larger and growing fast. Also, remember to take into account your soil type. Clay soils hold a lot more water for a much longer period of time than do sandy soils, which will require more frequent irrigation. (And remember, amending your soil each season with compost will keep it progressing toward that garden loam we all desire.)

If you do miss watering your plants, and they wilt, flood the plants with water as soon as you discover them. If they're not dry and dead, but just wilted, they should recover quickly, although the episode will set them back. Water them again deeply the next day, without waiting for the soil to dry out first. Keep them consistently watered thereafter.

Pests and Diseases

Insect pests aren't much of a problem when you grow cannabis outdoors. The only thing I've ever had trouble with is spider mites, which thrive in hot, dry conditions. I battle them every year. Keep a close eye out for their webs and the tiny mites on the undersides of leaves, beginning at the bottom of the plant and working up. Leaves start looking mottled or spotted with yellow if you have mites. If you suspect them, pluck a leaf and hold it up against the light, looking at it from the underside, or examine the leaves with a magnifying glass. This will make the red, brown, or black mites and their webs easier to spot.

If you find spider mites on your plants, spray with a mixture of Safer's Soap, an organic insecticide available at garden centers, and tobacco tea. I have been told that spraying with Neem, a product made from an Australian plant that is available where organic gardening products are carried, also works.

To prepare tobacco tea for an insecticide spray, place the tobacco from a three-quarter ounce package of loose tobacco into a one-gallon glass jar, and then fill the jar with boiling water and steep overnight. The next morning, strain the mixture through cheesecloth laid over a strainer or colander, and then pour the strained tobacco tea back into the rinsed jar for storage. (Specific directions for straining through cheesecloth can be found in chapter three, under the directions for making cannabis butter.) Keep the jar of tea, which will yield several batches of spray, in a cold, dark place such as the refrigerator.

To make the spray itself, place two cups of tobacco tea into a one-liter (or one quart) sprayer, add the amount of Safer's Soap called for in the package directions, and mix them together well. Fill the sprayer up the rest of the way with tepid water.

Initially, I spray three times in a row, three days apart, especially for a more advanced infestation. After that, I spray once every two weeks until the plants are in bloom, when I discontinue spraying. This will usually get them through the bloom cycle without being overtaken by spider mites. (I use the same schedule for pests on indoor plants, but I don't discontinue spraying, because those plants will not be entering bloom.) Take care to thoroughly cover the undersides of the leaves with spray.

Be *extremely* careful to spray only in the early morning, before bees and other beneficial insects are active, because this spray will kill any of them who come in contact with it. Spraying in the early morning also gives your plants plenty of time to dry out before cooler night-time temperatures, helping prevent disease and avoiding drawing slugs to the attack. And be careful not to inhale the spray, yourself. It won't be any better for you.

Some growers have reported problems with aphids, which are tiny, sucking insects large enough to be seen by the naked eye. Aphids are usually green, brown, black, or gray. They cluster around the tops of plants, on the undersides of leaves, and around tender new growth. If you find aphids on the leaves and stems, wash them off the plant with a firm spray of water. Check daily and continue doing this, which is all the intervention that aphids normally require. If they do become a greater problem, spray with Safer's Soap per package directions, using the same precautions I discussed above.

Animal pests such as rabbits and deer just need to be fenced out, as you do for the rest of your garden. Repellent sprays may work, but must be frequently reapplied. The most effective repellent spray I've found is based on mountain lion urine. Find these sprays in garden centers and garden catalogs.

Powdery mildew and bud rot are the main diseases to which cannabis is susceptible in my area. Powdery mildew is a fungal disease that looks like a white dusting of powder on the tops of leaves. It tends to be a problem when plants are too cold, too wet, or when there is not enough air circulation, so remember to address the underlying cause, as well as the mildew itself. If it's not controlled, leaves will gradually turn gray, wither, and die. The overall health of the plant will be harmed. Pick off affected leaves and discard *away* from the garden site. Never compost diseased foliage. Clean up diseased leaves on the ground around the plant and discard; this disease lives in soil. If the problem is severe or persistent, spray the foliage and surrounding ground once a week with a mixture of one tablespoon of baking soda mixed into one gallon of water. It helps if you add a couple of drops of organic dish soap or a commercial wetting agent. You can also use a commercial organic fungicide or antifungal agent.

Bud rot is another fungal disease. It manifests as a gray or brown rotten spot in your bud. Buds that grow extremely full and thick, or buds that get wet, are especially susceptible to rot. Fall rains may cause bud rot. If you find rot, and the bud is still immature, cut out the rot *immediately* with a very sharp pair of scissors, cutting into healthy tissue to be sure you get it all. Discard the diseased material. Dip your scissors into bleach, or use bleach wipes to sterilize them between cuts. Monitor the plant daily. Left alone, bud rot will quickly destroy the entire harvest. If the rot keeps returning and spreading, harvest the plant or the branch, even if it's not quite ready. That's better than losing it all. And keep watching—once I've discovered its presence, I've never found only one instance of bud rot.

(*Warning:* never smoke or ingest bud or any other plant material that contains rot. Always cut it completely out prior to drying and curing the herb. Inhaling the fungal spores can cause a very serious form of pneumonia. As far as I'm concerned, it's common sense not to eat diseased bud either.)

To help prevent disease, remove any lower branches that touch the ground (unless you're espaliering them there on purpose, of course). Keep the center of the plant opened up for decent air circulation by carefully spreading the main branches apart or by pruning out any branches that are small, crossing, or shaded by others. (I prune branches, rather than spread them apart, because this minimizes damage during storms; a plant with its branches spread breaks more easily.) Help prevent bud rot by not wetting developing buds. Allow the surface of the soil to dry between watering.

Remove large fan leaves when they yellow, if they become diseased, or if a leaf is shading a developing bud. Otherwise, leave them alone. It is not a good idea to routinely strip the plant of healthy fan leaves. These are feeder leaves and assist bud development by their presence.

Good, consistent, hygienic gardening practices and a healthy dose of common sense will go a long way toward minimizing any problems.

Chapter Four

Harvesting, Drying, and Curing

Determining maturity is an extremely subjective process. However, as a general rule, cannabis is ready to harvest when the buds feel firm, well formed, and plump when you squeeze them *gently,* and when about 50 percent of the stigmas have turned brown and withered. (See photographs.) However, be aware that stigmas can turn brown due to inclement weather, too; you have to be aware of what's going on around you. There are many ways to harvest and cure cannabis. Basically, I'm going to describe the methods that work for me. Feel free to adapt or personalize them to your own needs and preferences.

This bud is almost ready to harvest. Note that the stigmas haven't withered yet, but the bud is becoming plump and filled out.
(Photo courtesy of Jon Moore.)

This bud is mature and ready to harvest. Approximately 50 percent of the stigmas have withered, and the bud appears fully developed.
(Photo courtesy of Jon Moore.)

I harvest and clean one plant at a time to keep from mixing up varieties. I remove the whole plant at once by cutting each main stem, leaving a stump with a few bare branch ends sticking up. (Later, I go back out and dig, clean, and hang to dry any roots I plan to use for topical preparations, choosing roots from my strongest and healthiest plants.) I place the branches I cut into a bucket of water on the back porch and remove one stem at a time to clean. I find it easier to trim the buds if the plant has not yet wilted.

Cut a main branch down into its individual smaller branches. It's useful to trim each branch so you leave a hook at the end for hanging. (See photograph.) You accomplish this by leaving a bit of stem from another branch attached. Remove fan leaves and other larger leaves by hand if you are able to reach the base of the leaf stem to remove it without damaging the bud. Then trim off the parts of the rest of the leaves that are sticking out from the bud. Do not cut into the bud itself.

Note the hooks for hanging left at the ends of the branches.
(Photo courtesy of Jon Moore.)

Save the trimmings and small upper leaves to cook with and for topical preparations. I place them into a paper grocery bag as I work and then dry them in the same bag. I also drop very tiny, airy buds, the ones that will disappear to almost nothing when they dry, in with the other cooking material, rather than dealing with them individually. Leave the bag open and keep in a dark area. Turn and fluff the mass of vegetation in the bag once a day while it dries. Once it's dry, I place the paper bag full of dried herb into a plastic garbage bag and store it in the freezer.

When you've finished cleaning a plant, hang the buds from wires suspended from the ceiling. (See photograph.) Leave plenty of space between stems, and make sure you have good air circulation: run a fan if necessary. Temperatures should be between sixty and eighty degrees, and humidity should be moderate. Attach the plant label to the wire with a clothespin where one variety starts and another ends, or you will confuse your varieties. (Remember, I learned all this stuff the hard way; you don't have to.)

This medical cannabis is in the process of drying.
(Photo courtesy of Jon Moore.)

In order to achieve a good cure, buds should take one to two weeks to dry completely. I leave my cannabis buds hanging until the outsides of the buds feel very hard, but the stems still bend. I then move the branches into labeled paper grocery bags, cover with another bag, and dry in a dark place until the stems snap. This slows the drying process enough for a good cure.

Once your buds are dry, cut them off the stems to fit into storage containers, but don't cut into the buds themselves. Work over a tray to catch all the shake and kef that sift down as you work; they're excellent for cooking. Shake is the vegetative matter that falls off a bud whenever it is touched—the loose stuff you find in the bottom of the bag or container. Kef consists of trichomes that have been knocked off the surfaces of calyxes and leaves. Trichomes are the tiny crystals full of resin you can see covering mature buds that contain the medicinal components of cannabis.

Store the buds in airtight, labeled glass jars in a cool, dark place. Air, heat, and light degrade cannabinoids. Half-gallon or quart canning jars work well. If you absolutely cannot afford glass jars, use plastic freezer containers; just don't use plastic bags! Open the jars daily for the first month to check the condition of the buds and allow them to breathe. After that, just check once a month or so to make sure you don't have any rot or other problems starting.

You've done it—I told you that you could! Now settle back and enjoy the fruits of your labor!

PART III

Edible and Topical Preparations

Directions and recipes for cooking with the cannabis herb and for preparing topical applications follow. You can work with actual bud, with shake, with kef, or with leaves and bud clippings (trimmings). Hopefully, you can obtain organically grown cannabis for your use or are growing your own organically. The material can be green or dry; however, if you make butter with green herb, you will end up having to pour off water from the bottom after the butter solidifies.

Utilizing all parts of a plant when preparing herbal medicines, as can be done with cannabis, is holistic, respectful, and synergistically healing and balancing.

Chapter Five

Making Cannabis Edible

Cannabis Tincture

I obtained these directions from a physician specializing in cannabis medicine.

Tinctures may be administered directly under the tongue or can be diluted in tea, water, or juice. If you want to avoid ingesting the alcohol in the tincture, add the tincture to a little boiling water, remove the pan from the heat, and let it sit for five minutes uncovered to evaporate the alcohol. Start with a very small dose (e.g., one-half teaspoon), and adjust your dosage gradually until you achieve the results you desire.

Use a bit over one ounce of dry herb to one pint of 120-proof or stronger gin, vodka, brandy, or grain alcohol. Chop or grind the cannabis finely. Place in a clean, dry, glass jar, then pour the alcohol over the herbs until it is two to three inches above them. If the herbs swell and become uncovered, add more alcohol. Place the jar in a dark, cool place; stir daily with a glass or plastic implement for two weeks. After two weeks, uncover the jar to allow 10 to 20 percent of the alcohol to evaporate. Strain the remaining liquid through cheesecloth, as instructed for cannabis butter later in this part. Bottle the resulting liquid in a dark bottle, and label. Store in a cool, dark place.

Cannabis Capsules

These directions also came from a cannabis specialist.

Purchase empty capsules and liquid lecithin through a pharmacy or health food store, choosing a size of capsule you can swallow. Combine one gram of ground or powdered cannabis bud, one drop of liquid lecithin, and enough olive oil to make a somewhat dry paste. Stuff the bottom part of the capsule with this paste, put the capsule together, and store it in the refrigerator. One gram of cannabis should make about four capsules, depending upon the size of capsule you selected.

Cannabis Tea

Boil water. Add fresh or dried cannabis and steep for fifteen minutes. Some people use stems for tea, as well as leaves and bud. This tea is best combined with some other strong-flavored tea for better taste, such as peppermint or black tea. Add honey, sugar, or milk as desired.

Cannabis Butter: Method One

Use at least two cups of cannabis herb (bud, shake, trimmings, or kef) to each pound of butter (not margarine). I use organic butter and prepare four pounds at a time.

Melt butter in a large Crock-Pot (four quarts to six-and-one-half quarts). Chop or grind your herb, and add it to the melted butter. Cook on lowest setting of the Crock-Pot for four to six hours. If the liquid butter begins to bubble, creating trans-fatty acids, turn the pot off for about twenty minutes, then turn it on again; keep it on until the butter again begins to bubble. Repeat the procedure as needed. This heating and cooling minimizes the creation of trans-fatty acids and facilitates maximum extraction of the cannabinoids.

Turn off the Crock-Pot, and allow the mixture to cool until it is still liquid but able to be handled. Line a strainer or colander with cheesecloth (or use old, clean pantyhose). Set the strainer over a bowl or large measuring pitcher, and pour the cooled butter through the cheesecloth. Then, twist the top of the cheesecloth together over the cannabis pulp, and squeeze and wring until you cannot get any more melted butter out of the pulp. (Four pounds of butter should yield eight cups of liquid butter.) I wring the pulp by hand, but some friends of mine made wooden paddles to make it easier to squeeze or press out the herb. This is a good idea if arthritis or some other condition makes it difficult for you to do this by hand.

Dump the greasy cannabis pulp into a large saucepan, and either discard the cheesecloth or freeze it in a plastic bag to be heated in the microwave at a later date for use as a poultice. The pulp will be used to make a base for cannabis chocolate syrup (recipe follows).

Pour the strained green butter into pint canning jars, cool in the refrigerator until solid, then freeze. If you used four pounds of butter to make this recipe, you should have four one-pint jars of cannabis butter. Most of the cookie recipes that follow call for one of these pint jars of herbal butter, removing the necessity to measure the fat for the recipe.

Chocolate Syrup Base: Method One

This is a secondary product that is derived from the cannabis butter preparation. This recipe creates a cannabis-infused liquid from which you will make chocolate syrup. The chocolate syrup can be used on its own over ice cream or cake, or it can be used as a base for cocoa.

Pour boiling water to cover over the pulp you put in the saucepan. Bring back to a boil and then lower the heat to a low boil or simmer; cook, covered, for another two to four hours. Uncover the pan, raise the heat to high, and boil the liquid down until the liquid is concentrated to just below the level of the pulp. Cool, then strain the pulp through a new piece of cheesecloth as you did before. If you started with four pounds of butter when you initially made cannabis butter, you should end up with about eight cups of dark, green-brown liquid, with sediment on the bottom and a layer of cannabis butter on the top. Discard the pulp and the cheesecloth; neither should be very greasy. Pour the liquid into pint or quart jars, cool, and freeze. See below for actual chocolate syrup recipe.

Chocolate Syrup Base: Method Two

You can also choose to make this base alone, not as a secondary product of cannabis butter, if you have no need for butter. (*Warning:* this method yields a much more potent syrup. Be careful with dosage and start slowly.)

Melt two cubes (one cup) of butter in a large Crock-Pot. When the butter has melted, pour in a few cups of boiling water. Add chopped or ground herb (bud, shake, kef, or trimmings), filling the pot with the prepared cannabis to a couple of inches from the top. Cover everything with more boiling water to just above the level of the herbs. Cook on high until the mixture is boiling, then lower the heat to keep it simmering, and cook for four to six hours. Cool, strain, and process exactly as described for the original base.

Cannabis Butter: Method Two

My friend N, who shared this method with me, recommended that you use unsalted European butter because of its higher fat-to-water ratio. Due to the amount of herb used in this recipe, this method makes only one pound of butter at a time and may not be practical unless you grow your own cannabis.

Use one-half pound up to one-and-one-half pounds of cannabis herb to each pound of butter. N uses bud and does not chop or grind her cannabis. Melt the butter in a very large Crock-Pot, add the cannabis, then pour boiling water over until liquid is visible at the top of the cannabis. Cook four to six hours as described in method one. Cool and strain as described in method one. Pour the strained liquid into a bowl and refrigerate. The butter will solidify on the top of the liquid and can be pulled off. The liquid underneath is discarded. N often softens the resulting butter, enabling her to mold the flat disc into a more easily stored shape.

Cannabis Milk

If you want even stronger cocoa than you get from using the chocolate syrup alone, you can add a little cannabis milk. (Don't try to make cocoa with all cannabis milk; it tastes awful!) You can also use cannabis-infused milk for other beverages or in cooking.

Pour a half-gallon container of organic milk into a large saucepan, add two to four cups of cannabis herb, and heat at a low simmer, *without boiling*, for two to four hours. Cool and strain the green milk through cheesecloth as directed for cannabis butter. Pour into half-pint glass jars and freeze. Add one teaspoon up to two tablespoons of cannabis milk for each cup of milk or soymilk used for cocoa. Always start with the smaller amount and increase gradually until you achieve the desired effect.

Chapter Six

Cooking with Cannabis

Ingesting cannabis causes the compounds in it to be released slowly, as they're digested. The effect can take up to two hours to begin and can last four to eight hours or longer. It's better to begin by initially consuming a small amount, then gradually increasing the dose upward until the desired effect is obtained. For example, the first time you make cannabis cookies, begin with an initial dose of one-quarter of a cookie, and work up gradually. In my experience, individual dosages vary from one-quarter of a cookie to about three cookies. (These precautions also hold true for any other cannabis preparation that is ingested, including beverages, capsules, tinctures, and anything else you intend to take by mouth.) Finally, I have found that it works best to keep the cookies in the freezer once they're baked, removing and thawing only one day's dose at a time.

I also want to pass on some general information regarding cookie baking. I cool all my cookies on strips of unbleached parchment paper laid out on the kitchen table. This works well and is easy. I also line my cookie sheets with parchment paper, which can be purchased in grocery stores. The same paper can be used for multiple batches of cookies. The cookies bake without sticking, and there is virtually no clean up to do!

I personally use all organic ingredients and substitute Rapadura sugar (very dark brown and raw) for brown sugar, normal raw sugar for white sugar, and sea salt for regular salt. The sugars and sea salt can be purchased in health food stores. I use whole grain flours as much as possible. In my opinion, using healthier food strengthens and balances the body, allowing the cannabis in the preparations to heal more effectively; however, the recipes also work just fine with normal grocery shelf ingredients.

Cannabis Chocolate Syrup

Empty a quart jar (or two one-pint jars) of cold chocolate syrup base into a large saucepan. Add one-and-one-half cups of baking cocoa powder and one-and-one-half cups of sugar. Whisk in well and cook on a burner over medium-high heat, whisking or stirring constantly until the mixture reaches a boil that cannot be stirred down. Turn off the heat, and add one teaspoon of vanilla. Pour into a glass jar and refrigerate.

When you want a cup of cocoa, heat milk or soymilk in the microwave or on top of the stove to the desired temperature. Then stir in chocolate syrup until the mixture is as "chocolatey" as you like. To be safe, start with a fairly light cocoa, and increase the amount of syrup gradually until the desired effect has been reached. This is an excellent sleep aid, especially if soymilk is used.

Molasses Sugar Cookies

These cookies have great texture and a strong gingersnap flavor that adapts well to the taste of cannabis. Patients I know who have trouble handling the flavor of cannabis in baked goods can eat these.

1 one-pint jar (2 cups) cannabis butter, room temperature
2 cups sugar
½ cup molasses (blackstrap molasses is healthiest)
2 eggs
4 cups unbleached all-purpose flour (can be half whole wheat or white whole wheat, or a third whole barley flour)
4 teaspoons baking soda
2 teaspoons cinnamon
2 teaspoons ginger
1 teaspoon cloves
½ teaspoon salt

Cream cannabis butter and sugar well with an electric mixer. Add molasses and eggs, and beat until very well mixed, thick, and smooth. Sift or whisk together dry ingredients, and add to butter mixture, stirring just until mixed in well. Chill dough if it's difficult to work with.

Form into walnut-size balls, and roll in sugar. Place two inches apart on greased or parchment-paper-lined cookie sheets.

Bake at 375 degrees for nine to ten minutes. Cool slightly before removing from cookie sheet. Longer baking will make a crisper cookie, as opposed to chewy. Makes about six dozen.

Oatmeal Cookies: Method One

This recipe came from N, the same friend who shared her method for making cannabis butter. These taste really good and are easy and fast because they're based on a cookie mix.

Betty Crocker Oatmeal Cookie Mix
2 cups butterscotch chips
1 cup chopped walnuts
2 cups shredded coconut
1 pound or 2 cups cannabis butter, room temperature
1 tablespoon water (may have to add 1 or 2 tablespoons more)
1 egg

Add the other six ingredients to the cookie mix, adding more water if necessary for proper consistency. Bake at 375 degrees for nine to ten minutes, per box directions. Watch for burning due to using so much fat in the mix.

Oatmeal Cookies: Method Two

This recipe originally came from my mother and was adapted for medicinal use. She made these same cookies (without cannabis) for me when I was a child. Mother died in December, 2000, and I still miss her a *lot*. These cookies always remind me of her.

1 one-pint jar (2 cups) cannabis butter, room temperature
2 cups sugar
2 cups brown sugar
4 eggs
2 teaspoons vanilla
2 cups unbleached all-purpose flour (can be half whole wheat or white whole wheat, or a third whole barley flour)
2 teaspoons baking powder
1 teaspoon salt
2 teaspoons cinnamon
1 teaspoon nutmeg
6 cups uncooked, quick rolled oats

Place cannabis butter, sugars, eggs, and vanilla in mixing bowl of electric mixer, and beat thoroughly. Sift or whisk together dry ingredients, except for the oats. Add to butter mixture, and mix well. Stir in oats and any other ingredients you are adding.

Drop walnut-size spoonfuls two inches apart onto greased or parchment-paper-lined cookie sheets.

Bake at 350 degrees for eleven to twelve minutes. Cool slightly before removing from cookie sheet. Makes six to eight dozen.

(Can add raisins, dried cranberries, dates, other dried fruit, raw or toasted chopped nuts, chocolate chips, white chocolate chips, butterscotch chips, coconut, or whatever else sounds good to you.)

Old-Fashioned Chocolate Chip Cookies

I copied this recipe from my mother-in-law about thirty-five-years ago and have adapted it for medicinal use. Mom died a couple of years ago, but many of her recipes live on in our family.

1 one-pint jar (2 cups) cannabis butter, room temperature
1 cup sugar
1 cup brown sugar
2 eggs
2 teaspoons vanilla
2 teaspoons lemon juice (adds an unusual sparkle and depth of flavor)
3 cups unbleached all-purpose flour (can be half whole wheat or white whole wheat, or a third whole barley flour)
1 teaspoon baking soda
1 teaspoon salt
1 cup chopped nuts, raw or toasted
12-ounce package chocolate chips

Place cannabis butter, sugars, eggs, vanilla, and lemon juice in bowl of electric mixer, and beat thoroughly. Sift or whisk together dry ingredients. Add to butter mixture, and mix well. Stir in nuts and chocolate chips.

Drop walnut-size balls of dough two inches apart onto greased or parchment-paper-lined cookie sheets.

Bake at 375 degrees for eight to ten minutes, until light brown. Cool slightly before removing from cookie sheet. Makes five dozen.

(Can substitute chunks of a candy bar for part or all of the chocolate chips. Can also use white chocolate chips in part or in all, and can leave out the nuts. Add melted semisweet chocolate for double chocolate chip cookies.)

Cocoa Snowflakes

This is actually a traditional Christmas cookie, but it lends itself very well to medicinal use. The cookies taste like bite-size, chewy brownies coated in powdered sugar.

2 cups unbleached all-purpose flour
2 teaspoons baking powder
½ teaspoon salt
⅔ cup cannabis butter, room temperature (Yes, you actually have to measure it!)
¾ cup baking cocoa powder
2 cups sugar
2 teaspoons vanilla
4 eggs
1 cup powdered sugar in which to roll cookies

Sift together flour, baking powder, and salt, and set aside.

In a small, heavy saucepan, melt cannabis butter over low heat. Whisk in the cocoa powder until smooth. Remove pan from heat, and stir in sugar until combined. You should have a very dark brown mixture at this point.

Transfer cocoa mixture to a large mixing bowl. Add vanilla extract, then eggs, one at a time, stirring well by hand or with a hand mixer after each addition. Add flour mixture. (Using a hand mixer is by far the easier thing to do.)

Cover the dough and refrigerate until chilled and able to be worked.

Remove enough dough from the refrigerator at one time to fill one cookie sheet, allowing the remainder to stay chilled. Roll into walnut-size balls. Roll balls in powdered sugar. Try coating your hands with powdered sugar if the dough is sticking to them.

Place the balls of dough two inches apart on a greased or parchment-paper-lined cookie sheet.

Bake at 400 degrees for eight minutes. Be careful that the bottoms of the cookies don't burn. (Using parchment paper and/or double-walled cookie sheets will just about eliminate this problem.) Cool slightly before removing from cookie sheet. Makes six dozen.

You can add finely chopped raw or toasted nuts, if you like nuts in your brownies.

Peanut Butter Cookies

This is another recipe I copied from Mom over thirty years ago and have adapted for medicinal use. These cookies are delicious!

1 one-pint jar (2 cups) cannabis butter, room temperature
2 cups natural peanut butter, such as Adams or Arrowhead Mills (does not contain sugar or shortening)
2 cups sugar
2 cups brown sugar
4 eggs
2 teaspoons vanilla
5 cups unbleached all-purpose flour (can be half whole wheat or white whole wheat, or a third whole barley flour)
1 tablespoon baking soda
1 teaspoon salt

Beat butters together with an electric mixer. Beat in sugars until fluffy and light colored. Add eggs and vanilla. Sift or whisk together dry ingredients, and add to butter mixture.

Drop walnut-size balls of dough two inches apart onto a greased or parchment-paper-lined cookie sheet. Press dough balls flat in a crisscross pattern with the floured or sugared tines of a fork.

Bake at 375 degrees for nine to eleven minutes, until brown and crisp. Cool slightly before removing from cookie sheet. Makes eight dozen.

Toasted, salted peanuts, chopped or whole (or anything chocolate), are an excellent addition to these cookies.

Chapter Seven

Topical Preparations

Cannabis Oil (edible or topical use)

I obtained this recipe from my friend, Judy Ryland, who is highly respected in the natural healing and medical cannabis communities in our area. She recommended using organic sesame oil for a base in this recipe, explaining that sesame oil is deeply penetrating, with antifungal and antimicrobial properties. Topically, cannabis oil is used for joint and muscle pain, as well as bruises. It is very helpful for arthritis. It has also been reported to ease psoriasis. If you are *not* going to ingest this oil, you can add essential oils such as wintergreen or chamomile to complement the anti-inflammatory effects of the cannabis alone. If you do not add any essential oils, you can use the oil for cooking as you would any other oil, although it is usually used topically.

Place two cups of green or dry cannabis herb into a clean, dry jar, and cover with oil. Using dry herb will allow you to concentrate it better in the oil, because you can put more in. Cover the jar, and keep it in a dark place for six weeks up to one year. When you are ready to use the oil, strain it through cheesecloth or pantyhose as directed for cannabis butter. Continue to store it in a dark, cool place; the refrigerator is good. You can warm the oil prior to using it.

Cannabis Root Liniment (external use only)

Cannabis root is replete with anti-inflammatory components, but contains no THC. This is an old folk remedy for joint and muscle pain that really works!

Chop a fresh or dried cannabis root into small pieces. (Be prepared; it's tough. Use a large butcher knife or sharp kitchen shears.) Place the chopped root into a saucepan. Cover with water. Bring to a boil and boil, covered, for four to six hours. Uncover the pan at the end of this time and boil briskly until the liquid has concentrated down to just below the level of the chopped root. Strain, and store the resulting golden liquid in half-pint glass jars in the freezer. When you need liniment, add a one-pint bottle (sixteen fluid ounces) of rubbing alcohol to a half-pint jar of cannabis root base. Store the prepared liniment in a dark cupboard. Shake well before using, and apply as needed.

Cannabis Root Oil (external use only)

I saw the cannabis root prepared this way while attending the 2006 NORML conference in San Francisco. A couple had laid out an intriguing display demonstrating the various uses of both medicinal and hemp cannabis. The quart jar in the demonstration was packed with pieces of cannabis root, as one would pack pickles or whole carrots into a jar for canning. This is another preparation that is full of anti-inflammatory elements. It is excellent for joint and muscle pain or strain and for bruising.

Clean and cut up enough cannabis root to fit into the jar you are going to use, keeping the pieces of root as whole as possible. (Scrub the roots very well.) Place them into a clean, dry jar, and cover with organic sesame oil or other organic oil of your choice. Cover the jar, and store in a cool, dark place for at least six weeks up to six months. No need to remove the root before using the oil unless it begins to look bad; then just strain it out of the oil. Storage in the refrigerator is best. Warm the oil prior to using.

PART IV

Cautions and Conclusions

Chapter Eight

Just Say Know

I believe it has been definitively demonstrated that *Cannabis sativa* is a beneficial and medicinal plant. The menace that has been claimed for it derives not from its inherent properties, but from its political and legal status. Few medicines, natural or synthetic, treat so much so safely and so well. Cannabis offers an opportunity for balance and health to a world that desperately needs balancing and healing. It is up to us to accept the offer.

However, you must still determine if medical cannabis is an appropriate option for you. In addition to medical considerations, two items should heavily influence your decision: federal law and your state's laws regarding the use of cannabis for medicine. The DEA and the federal government do not officially recognize any valid medical use for cannabis, whether or not this attitude has a scientific (or even honest) basis. Federally, cannabis is an illegal substance. Although the DEA appears to be focusing its primary efforts on large grows and commercial operations, not individual medical cannabis patients operating within their respective laws and guidelines, this situation can (and sometimes does) change. Be aware of the risks. As I recently heard a physician caution a new medical cannabis patient, "You now have legal permission to use a medicine that's still illegal."

If you do not live in a state that has legalized the use of cannabis for medicine, I cannot recommend that you grow or use cannabis at all; you would be engaging in a purely illegal activity. If your state has provided for medical use, know your state and local laws and guidelines, and comply with them. If you do not know what your guidelines and laws are, contact the office of your district attorney, local law enforcement, or go to ASA's Web site: http://www.safeaccessnow.org/. If medical cannabis is not legal in your state, ASA can show you ways to work to change that law.

You can also become involved with the medical cannabis community in your area. Smaller groups, such as the El Dorado County

American Alliance for Medical Cannabis (AAMC), are often able to work very effectively within their communities and with local law enforcement to establish clear and fair guidelines for medical cannabis patients. Such groups are also sources of education, patient advocacy and support, and community service. (For example, the AAMC sponsors a blood pressure monitoring booth in Garden Valley Park every Fourth of July and participates in the holiday food drive conducted by the local Grange.) If you want more information about starting your own group, the national AAMC Web site (http://www.letfreedomgrow.com/) has an article written by my friend, Dave Bishop, on this subject. Remember, there is strength in numbers. You can be an effective agent for positive change within your community.

So, if you use cannabis medically, and especially if you grow your own medicine, do so intelligently and with appropriate caution. Know all the rules, and stringently follow them. Know your state and local guidelines, and stay within them. Know the recommendations of your physician, and comply with them. Know what documentation you need to have, and have it. Know what to do if the police come knocking on your door, and be ready to do it. Use common sense. Educate yourself. Know your risks; know your local law enforcement; and know your community.

Or, as my friend Dave says, "Just say *know*."

May your path be clear, your day bright, and your journey joyful!

978-0-595-45086-2
0-595-45086-5